Sunset Boulevard was first performed at the Adelphi Theatre
on 12th July 1993. The cast was as follows:

NORMA DESMOND	Patti LuPone
JOE GILLIS	Kevin Anderson
MAX MAYERLING	Daniel Benzali
BETTY SCHAEFER	Meredith Braun
CECIL B. DEMILLE	Michael Bauer
ARTIE GREEN	Gareth Snook
MANFRED	Nicolas Colicos
SHELDRAKE	Harry Ditson
Director	Trevor Nunn
Music	Andrew Lloyd Webber

SUNSET BOULEVARD

THE MUSICAL

Don Black and Christopher Hampton

MUSIC BY
Andrew Lloyd Webber

BASED ON THE SCREENPLAY BY
Billy Wilder, Charles Brackett
and D. M. Marshman, Jr.

faber and faber
LONDON · BOSTON

First published in 1993 by
Faber and Faber Limited
3 Queen Square London WC1N 3AU

Photoset by Parker Typesetting Service, Leicester
Printed in England by Clays Ltd, St Ives plc

A CIP record of this book is available from the British Library

ISBN 0-571-17214-8

2 4 6 8 10 9 7 5 3 1

ACT ONE

I: THE HOUSE ON SUNSET

The patio and exterior of a preposterous, Italianate
Hollywood mansion, not more than twenty years old, but
already shabby from neglect. The deep end of the swimming
pool is visible, the rest stretching off into the wings. Floating
in the pool, fully clothed, face down, is the body of a young
man. Dawn is just beginning to break.

Over this image, once it has become established, the voice
of JOE GILLIS.

JOE (*Voice over*)
I guess it was five a.m.
A homicide had been reported
From one of those crazy mansions
Up on Sunset.
Tomorrow every front page
Is going to lead with this story;
You see an old time movie star is involved
Maybe the biggest star of all.
(*By now, a handsome, broad-shouldered man in his early*
thirties has emerged from the crowd and moved downstage
to address the audience directly: this is JOE GILLIS.)
JOE
But before you read about it,
Before it gets distorted
By those Hollywood piranhas,
If you want to know the real facts
You've come to the right party.
(*During this, the stage is irregularly raked by cold blue light*

I

which turns out to be thrown by the L.A.P.D. patrol cars, one of which draws up and disgorges a number of POLICEMEN, *who split up; two approach the house, while another two move over to contemplate the body in the pool.)*

2: PARAMOUNT

The gates and open areas at the front of the Paramount lot, leading to the studios and the administration blocks. It is morning and a variety of young hopefuls are milling about in the forecourt, waiting for their interviews, assignments or auditions, and trying to impress one another. As this world gradually assembles before our eyes, JOE's *tone changes; he continues to address the audience.*

JOE
    Let me take you back six months.
    I was at the bottom of the barrel,
    I'd had a contract down at Fox
    But I'd fallen foul of Darryl.
    I had a date at Paramount,
    Along with about a thousand other writers.
    If this didn't come up roses
    I'd be covering funerals
    Back in Dayton, Ohio.
    I'd hidden my car three blocks away.
    Turned out to be a smart move.
    (JOE *approaches the gate, where he's challenged by* JONES, *the elderly guard.)*
JOE
    I have an appointment with Mr Sheldrake.
JONES
    Name?

2

JOE

Gillis. Joseph Gillis.

(JONES *consults his clipboard. Meanwhile,* JOE's *name has caught the attention of two men in hats and bad suits: the* FINANCE MEN.)

JONES

OK.

(*He waves* JOE *through and* JOE *joins the young hopefuls: these include* MYRON, *a director;* MARY, *a young actress, blonde and beautiful, artfully dishevelled;* JOANNA, *a writer, dark and intense;* CLIFF, *a cameraman; and* KATHERINE, *a willowy, pale New York actress. They weave in and out of the technicians shifting heavy equipment and the costumed extras, greeting each other with air-kisses, casual waves and ritualized exchanges.*)

JOE

Hi there, Myron.

MYRON

How's it hanging?

JOE

I've got a date with Sheldrake.

MYRON

I'm shooting a western down at Fox.

JOE

How can you work with Darryl?

MYRON

We should talk.

JOE

Gotta run.

BOTH

Let's have lunch.

MARY

Hi, Mr Gillis.

JOE
  You look great.
MARY
  I'm up for an audition.
JOE
  Sheldrake is driving me insane.
MARY
  Don't forget me when you're casting.
JOE
  We should talk.
MARY
  Gotta run.
JOE
  Let's have lunch.

JOE
  Morning, Joanna.
JOANNA
  Hi, how're you doing?
JOE
  I've got a date with Sheldrake.
JOANNA
  I'm handing in my second draft.
JOE
  I'd really love to read it.
JOANNA
  We should talk.
JOE
  Gotta run.
BOTH
  Let's have lunch.

  (*Simultaneous with the above:*)
MARY
  Hi there, Myron.

4

MYRON
  How's it hanging?
MARY
  I'm up for an audition.
MYRON
  I'm shooting a western down at Fox.
MARY
  Don't forget me when you're casting.
MYRON
  We should talk.
MARY
  Gotta run.
BOTH
  Let's have lunch.
  (*As he moves away from* JOANNA, JOE *is suddenly waylaid
  by the* FINANCE MEN.)
FIRST FINANCE MAN
  We want the keys to your car.
SECOND FINANCE MAN
  You're way behind with the payments.
FIRST FINANCE MAN
  Don't give us any fancy footwork . . .
SECOND FINANCE MAN
  Give us the keys.
JOE
  I only wish I could help.
  I loaned it to my accountant.
  He has an important client down in Palm Springs,
  Felt like playing some golf.
FIRST FINANCE MAN
  Are you telling us you walked here?
JOE
  I believe in self-denial.
  I'm in training for the priesthood.

SECOND FINANCE MAN
OK, wise guy. Three hundred bucks.
FIRST FINANCE MAN
Or we're taking the car.
SECOND FINANCE MAN
We have a court order.
JOE
I love it when you talk dirty.
(*He slips away from them, back into the social whirl. The* FINANCE MEN *meanwhile, by no means convinced, settle down to watch and wait. A* GRIP, *struggling with a huge papier-mâché totem pole, encounters a* MAKE-UP GIRL, *hurrying in the opposite direction.*)

CLIFF
Where've you been hiding?
JOE
What are you shooting?
CLIFF
Trying to make my mind up.
GRIP
Why don't you ever call me back?
(*The* MAKE-UP GIRL *hurries on without answering.*)
CLIFF
Hey, isn't that your agent?
JOE
We should talk.
CLIFF
Gotta run.
BOTH
Let's have lunch.

(*Simultaneous with the above:*)
JOANNA
Hi there, Mary.

6

MARY
  How're you doing?
JOANNA
  Writing for Betty Hutton.

MARY
  I'm up for something really big.
JOANNA
  Shouldn't you undo a button?
MARY
  We should talk.
JOANNA
  Gotta run.
BOTH
  Let's have lunch.
  (JOE *moves swiftly towards a sharply-dressed middle-aged man,* MORINO, *his agent.* MORINO *is with a very much younger man and does his best to pretend not to notice* JOE. *When he realizes the encounter is unavoidable, he makes a great show of pleasurable surprise and greets* JOE *with effusive bonhomie.*)
MORINO
  Greetings, Gillis.
  What brings you here?
JOE
  You're the one who fixed the date.
MORINO
  Make it quick, don't keep us waiting.
  We're with Sheldrake
  10.15.
JOE
  Who is this?
MORINO
  He's my new boy.

BOY

I have a play on Broadway.

MORINO

In verse. Every major studio is . . .

JOE (*Interrupting*)

I need 200 dollars.

MORINO (*To his boy*)

He's always been a joker.

JOE

OK, 100. I really need some money.

MORINO

Maybe what you need is a new agent.

(*He turns his back on* JOE, *puts his arm around his new boy and moves off, murmuring in his ear.* JOE *watches them for a second, then checks his watch and continues his progress through the constantly developing ballet of salutations. An instrumental section, during which a* GRIP *makes his way towards one of the studio buildings, carrying a step-ladder.*)

GRIP

What can I tell you? It's for Alan Ladd's love-scene.

(*A group of extras from Cecil B. DeMille's latest extravaganza, 'Samson and Delilah', crosses the stage:* JOE *thinks he recognizes a man with a false beard and gold helmet who's accompanied by a gaggle of scantily-clad dancing girls:* SAMMY. *The latter raises his hand in a priestly gesture.*)

SAMMY

Bless you, Joseph.

JOE

That you, Sammy?

SAMMY

How do you like my harem?

JOE

How come you get such lousy breaks?

SAMMY
One learns to grin and bear 'em.
GIRLS
This is the
Biggest film
Ever made.
JOE
What're you playing?
FIRST GIRL
Temple virgin.
SECOND GIRL
Handmaiden to Delilah.
JOE
Let's have lunch.
(JOE *spots another friend of his,* ARTIE GREEN, *a fresh-faced assistant director in his mid-twenties.*)
JOE
Hello, Artie.
ARTIE
Joe, you bastard!
JOE
You never call me any more.
ARTIE
Found a cuter dancing-partner.
How are things?
JOE
Not so great.
ARTIE
Will this help?
(*He hands* JOE *a 20-dollar bill;* JOE *hesitates, then accepts it.*)
JOE
Thanks, you're a pal. I'll pay you back.
ARTIE
When you sign your contract.

(JOE *nods, pats* ARTIE *on the shoulder and moves on. The ceremony of empty greetings builds up contrapuntally, as* JOE *suddenly becomes isolated by a light in the midst of it all. He shakes his head, as if to clear a headache, as the intricate cacophony swells around him and the* CHORUS *works through its ritual exchanges:*)

CHORUS (*Separate voices*)

Morning, Joanna.

Where've you been hiding?

How're you doing?

Hi there, Katherine.

I hate this weather.

You look great.

We should talk.

What're you doing?

I'm trying to make my mind up.

Guess I was born to play her.

What is my motivation?

Gotta run.

They're talking nominations.

Is your new script with Sheldrake?

I'm very close to Sheldrake.

We shoot next month.

I just signed.

Let's have lunch.

R.K.O. are OK.

Let's drive to Vegas this weekend.

I'm handing in my second draft.

It's between me and Dietrich.

I've landed a big Broadway show.

I'm going to work for Metro.

I'd really love to read it.

I'd know just how to light you.

Let's pencil in Thursday morning.

This is the biggest film ever made!

CHORUS (*All*)
>Hi, good morning.
>Aren't we lucky?
>Going to work with Cukor.
>Paramount is paradise
>Movies from A to Zukor.
>We should talk
>Gotta run.
>Let's have lunch.
>(*Meanwhile, the lights have come up on* SHELDRAKE's
>*office.* SHELDRAKE, *a mournful dyspeptic figure, sits
>behind a big desk, innocent of books, speaking into one of
>his array of phones.*)

SHELDRAKE
>This is Sheldrake.
>Get me that shithead, Nolan.
>(*A total change of tone:*)
>Nolan, sweetheart, great to talk,
>I read your script this morning
>It won't work.
>It won't work.
>Who needs lunch?
>(SHELDRAKE *is shaking some bicarb into a tumbler of
>water and stirring it as* JOE *is shown into his office. He
>looks up, surprised, and makes an unconvincing stab at
>conviviality.*)

SHELDRAKE
>Joe! What the hell brings you here?

JOE
>You wanted to see me.

SHELDRAKE
>Did I?
>(*He thinks for a moment, frowning ferociously, and downs
>his medicine.*)

SHELDRAKE
  Any idea what about?
JOE
  I sent you an outline.
SHELDRAKE
  You did? I never saw it. Nobody tells me anything.
JOE
  'Bases Loaded'. It's a baseball story.
SHELDRAKE
  So pitch.
JOE
  It's about a rookie shortstop that's batting 347. The kid
  was once mixed up in a hold-up. Now he's trying to go
  straight, only . . .
SHELDRAKE
  Wait a minute, I think I have read this.
  (*He presses a buzzer on the intercom on his desk.*)
SHELDRAKE
  Can somebody bring in whatever we have on . . .
  (*He looks up at* JOE, *hoping for guidance.*)
JOE
  'Bases Loaded'.
SHELDRAKE
  . . . 'Bases Loaded'?
  (*He puts down the receiver, turns his attention back to*
  JOE.)
SHELDRAKE
  They tell the kid he has to throw the World Series, am I
  right?
JOE
  They're pretty hot for it over at Twentieth.
SHELDRAKE
  Good!
JOE
  No, I don't trust Zanuck. Can you see Ty Power as a

shortstop? You've got the best man for it right here on the
lot: Alan Ladd.
(*There's a knock and* BETTY SCHAEFER *steps into the
room. She's a clean-cut, bright-looking girl in her twenties.
She advances on* SHELDRAKE, *dropping a folder on his
desk, not noticing* JOE.)

BETTY

Here's that 'Bases Loaded' material, Mr Sheldrake. I made
a two-page synopsis of it for you. But I wouldn't bother to
read it.

SHELDRAKE

Why not?

BETTY

It's just a rehash of something that wasn't very good to
begin with.

SHELDRAKE

Meet Mr Gillis. He wrote it.
(BETTY *turns to* JOE, *horribly embarrassed.*)

SHELDRAKE

This is Miss Kramer.

BETTY

Schaefer. Betty Schaefer. And right now, I'd like to crawl
into a hole and pull it in after me.

JOE

If I could be of any help . . .

BETTY

I'm sorry, Mr Gillis, I couldn't see the point of it. I think
pictures should at least try to say a little something.

JOE

I see, you're one of the message kids. I expect you'd have
turned down *Gone with the Wind*.

SHELDRAKE

No, that was me.

BETTY

And I guess I was disappointed. I've read some of the stories you wrote for the magazines and I thought you had some real talent.

JOE

That was last year. This year I felt like eating.

BETTY

Well, I'm sorry, Mr Gillis.

JOE

Next time I'll write you *The Naked and the Dead*.

SHELDRAKE

Thank you, Miss Kramer.

(BETTY *leaves the room.* SHELDRAKE *looks up at* JOE.)

SHELDRAKE

Looks like Darryl's got himself a baseball picture.

JOE

Have you got any kind of work?

SHELDRAKE

There's nothing. Unless . . . we're always looking for a Betty Hutton. Suppose we made it a girl softball team? Throw in a few numbers. Might make a cute musical.

JOE

Are you trying to be funny? Because I'm all out of laughs. I'm over a barrel. I need a job. Additional dialogue. Anything.

SHELDRAKE

Something may come up. I'll keep you in mind.

JOE

Listen, Mr Sheldrake, could you let me have 300 dollars? As a personal loan?

(SHELDRAKE *is dreadfully taken aback. His hand goes to his solar plexus.*)

JOE

I've been grinding out original stories, two a week, for months now. Maybe they're not original enough. Maybe they're too original.

SHELDRAKE

   The finest things in the world have been written on an
   empty stomach.

JOE

   It's not my stomach I'm worried about, it's my car. If I lose
   that in this town, it's like having my legs cut off.
   (*The phone rings and* SHELDRAKE *jumps at the
   opportunity to take the call.*)

SHELDRAKE

   Yes . . . OK . . . put him on.
   (*He turns back to* JOE.)
   The thing is, last year some bastard talked me into buying a
   ranch in the valley . . .
   (*Back to the phone.*)
   Well, who does he have in mind?
   (*Back to* JOE.)
   And this year I had to mortgage the ranch so I could keep
   up my life insurance payments . . .
   (*He turns back to the phone;* JOE *gives up and walks out on
   him.*)
   Brando? Brando? Take it from me, nobody wants to see
   that Brando kid.
   (*He turns back to continue his spiel; but* JOE *has vanished.*)
   (BETTY SCHAEFER *hurries after* JOE *and catches him up.*)

JOE

   Come to get your knife back? It's still here, right between
   my shoulder blades.

BETTY

   You wrote a story, a couple of years back. About a teacher.
   Title something to do with windows.

JOE

   Blind Windows.

BETTY

   I really liked it.

15

JOE

You're making me feel all warm and runny inside.

BETTY

Maybe I can get Sheldrake to option it.
(*Silence.* JOE *glances at the* FINANCE MEN, *circling like sharks.*)

JOE

I doubt it. He likes pictures with great weather and happy endings.

BETTY

Why don't you let me try?
(JOE *considers for a moment, tempted, hesitating.*)
Let's get together.

JOE

That's what they all say.

BETTY

I'll be at Schwab's on Thursday.
I'm always there round six o'clock.

JOE

I gotta check my diary.

BETTY

We should talk.

JOE

Gotta run.

BETTY

What's the rush?
Why don't you
Stay awhile?

JOE

See those gorillas?

BETTY

Yes, what about them?

JOE

Do me a terrific favour.
Keep them amused while I escape.

BETTY
   If you'll agree to Thursday.
   (JOE *hesitates fractionally.*)
JOE
   Done.
FIRST FINANCE MAN
   Come on, show us
   Where you parked it.
SECOND FINANCE MAN
   Or I'll reshape your face.
BETTY
   Would you like to go on the set of Samson and Delilah?
FIRST FINANCE MAN
   No.
BETTY
   I think Mr DeMille is shooting one of Hedy's red hot
   scenes today.
SECOND FINANCE MAN
   I think we maybe have five minutes.
   (*She leads them through a tall doorway and ingeniously*
   vanishes, leaving them disorientated for a moment. Then
   they simultaneously realize they've been tricked and set off
   back towards their car at a run.)

                    3:ON THE ROAD

JOE'*s car noses into one of the main boulevards near*
Paramount; but the FINANCE MEN *come roaring up in*
pursuit. JOE *hits the gas and a high speed chase ensues.*
Finally after a hair-raising dash through the Holmby Hills,
JOE'*s car turns on to Sunset, gains some distance with an*
enterprising U-turn and then suffers a sudden blow-out.
With some difficulty, JOE *manages to control the car and*
turns into an open driveway, which then curves away from

the street, so that the FINANCE MEN *thunder by without seeing* JOE'*s car.*

4:THE HOUSE ON SUNSET

The property is noticeably shabbier and more run-down than it was in the opening scene. The patio and a little formal garden are choked with weeds, the plants on the balcony are overgrown and out of control and the pool is covered over. JOE *jumps out of his car.*

JOE

What a lovely sight: a great big empty garage.
(*He pushes his car the last few yards into the garage; and discovers that it's not empty after all. Under a tarpaulin, which* JOE *lifts, curious, is the rear of an insanely elaborate 1932 Isotta-Fraschini. He contemplates it for a moment.*)

JOE

This must burn up ten gallons to a mile.
(*He emerges from the garage and starts walking up towards the house. He comes to a halt, marvelling both at the scale and the dereliction of the house.*)

JOE

Christ, where am I?
I had landed
In the driveway of some palazzo,
Like an abandoned movie set.
(*Suddenly he is startled by a sharp, decisive woman's voice, cutting harshly into his reverie. He looks up at the balcony above but no one is visible.*)

VOICE

You there!
(JOE *approaches, still searching in vain for the source of the voice.*)

VOICE

Why are you so late?

(*Before he can summon up an answer, another shock; the French doors grind open and an extraordinary figure emerges from the house. This is* MAX MAYERLING, *a sixty-year-old butler in black tail coat, striped trousers, stiff-collar shirt and white cotton gloves. He contemplates* JOE, *his expression blank; then speaks in some mitteleuropäisch accent.*)

MAX

This way.

(JOE *steps forward, responding to* MAX's *natural authority.*)

MAX

And wipe your feet!

(JOE *obeys and steps through the French doors into a huge, gloomy drawing-room. The floor is tiled and the ceiling supported with dark heavy beams. There are framed photographs everywhere and musty hangings. The breeze moans through the pipes of a built-in organ. At the back of the room, on a massage table, something is lying, shrouded in a Spanish shawl, with candles in silver candlesticks burning at each corner of the table. The* VOICE *rings out again from above, where a black marble staircase leads up to a broad gallery.*)

VOICE

Max! Tell him to wait!

(MAX *turns to* JOE, *his tone chilly.*)

MAX

You heard.

(*He starts to move off.*)

MAX

If you need my help with the coffin, call me.

JOE

Just a minute . . .

(But MAX *is gone.* JOE *looks around, somewhat at a loss. But before he can make a move, the door to the gallery opens and another bizarre figure appears:* NORMA DESMOND. *Despite the gloom, she's wearing dark glasses and she's dressed in black loose pyjamas and black high heel pumps. She looks younger than her age, which is probably somewhere in the vicinity of fifty and, despite a sickly pallor, she's extremely striking and was evidently once a great beauty. Her hair is encased in a leopardskin-patterned chiffon scarf.* JOE *watches her, transfixed, as she proceeds in a stately fashion down the stairs.)*

NORMA

Any laws against burying him in the garden?

JOE

I wouldn't know.

NORMA

I don't care anyway.

(She sweeps past him to the back of the room, where she stands for a moment looking down at the child-sized bundle on the massage table. JOE, *all his writer's instincts now alerted, watches her, fascinated.)*

NORMA

No more wars to fight.
White flags fly tonight.
You are out of danger now.
Battlefield is still,
Wild poppies on the hill.
Peace can only come when you surrender.
Here the tracers fly,
Lighting up the sky
But I'll fight on to the end.
Let them send their armies;
I will never bend.
I won't see you now till I surrender.
I'll see you again when I surrender.

20

(*As the last echoes of this die away, she sweeps up the corpse into her arms, the shawl falls away and for the first time, we see the body is that of a chimpanzee.* NORMA *stares defiantly at* JOE, *the monkey's face cradled against her own.*)

NORMA

Now don't you give me a fancy price, just because I'm rich.

JOE

Lady, you've got the wrong man.

(NORMA *pauses in the act of rearranging the corpse and shoots* JOE *a fierce glance.*)

JOE

I had some trouble with my car, I just pulled into your driveway.

NORMA

Get out.

JOE

OK. And I'm sorry you lost your friend.

NORMA

Get out of here.

(JOE's *almost out: then he turns back, frowning.*)

JOE

Haven't I seen you somewhere before?

NORMA

Or shall I call my servant?

JOE

Aren't you Norma Desmond? You used to be in pictures. You used to be big.

NORMA

I am big. It's the pictures that got small.

(*She advances on him, flushed with indignation.*)

NORMA

There was a time in this business
You wouldn't remember.
We had the eyes of the whole wide world

But that wasn't good enough
For those Einsteins in the front office,
They wanted the ears of the world as well.
So they took all the idols and smashed them.
The Fairbanks, the Gilberts, the Valentinos.
They trampled on what was divine.
They threw away the gold of silence.
When all they needed was this face of mine.

JOE

Don't blame me, I'm just a writer.

(JOE's *back in the room now; watching as* NORMA *summons up before him the essence of her vanished stardom.*)

NORMA

With one look
I can break your heart,
With one look
I play every part.
I can make your sad heart sing,
With one look you'll know
All you need to know.
With one smile
I'm the girl next door,
Or the love that you've hungered for.
When I speak it's with my soul,
I can play any role.
No words can tell
The stories my eyes tell,
Watch me when I frown.
You can't write that down.
You know I'm right,
It's there in black and white.
When I look your way
You'll hear what I say.
Yes, with one look

I put words to shame.
Just one look
Sets the screen aflame.
Silent music starts to play;
One tear from my eye
Makes the whole world cry.
With one look
They'll forgive the past.
They'll rejoice: I've returned at last
To my people in the dark,
Still out there in the dark . . .
(*She sweeps majestically around the stage, as the orchestra takes the melody.*)

NORMA

Silent music starts to play,
With one look you'll know
All you need to know.
With one look
I'll ignite a blaze,
I'll return to my glory days.
They'll say Norma's back at last.
This time I'm staying,
I'm staying for good.
I'll be back
Where I was born to be.
With one look
I'll be me.
(*She comes to herself suddenly, aware once again of his presence.*)

NORMA

Now go.
(JOE *nods good-naturedly, turns and sets off towards the French doors. He's almost out of them, when* NORMA *speaks again.*)

NORMA
 Just a minute.
 (JOE *stops in the doorway, half turns back.*)
NORMA
 Did you say you were a writer?
JOE
 That's what it says on my Guild card.
NORMA
 And you've written pictures?
JOE
 Sure have. Would you like to see my credits?
NORMA
 Come over here, I want to ask you something.
 (JOE *hesitates; but his curiosity gets the better of him and*
 he begins to move back into the body of the room.)
NORMA
 What sort of length is a movie script these days?
JOE
 Depends.
 (*Standing by the sofa, next to the gold grand piano*
 covered in photographs, is an immense manuscript, several
 bundles, each wrapped in red ribbon, standing about two
 feet high.)
NORMA
 I wrote this. It's a very important picture.
JOE
 Looks like six very important pictures.
NORMA
 It's for DeMille to direct.
JOE
 Oh, yeah? And will you be in it?
NORMA
 Of course. What do you think?
JOE
 Just asking. I didn't know you were planning a comeback.

NORMA

I hate that word. It's a return.

JOE

Fair enough.

NORMA

I want you to read it.
(*This takes* JOE *by surprise; it takes him a moment to devise a response.*)

JOE

You shouldn't let another writer read your stuff. He may steal it.

NORMA

I'm not afraid. Sit down. Max!
(JOE *still dithers;* MAX *appears at once.*)

NORMA

Bring something to drink.

MAX

Yes, Madame.
(JOE *brightens; but still hesitates.*)

NORMA

I said sit down!
(JOE *lapses on to the sofa. The following sequence telescopes the passing of time covered by the reading of the script; but for now,* NORMA, *with great care, picks up the first of the bundles of manuscript, almost sensually slips off the ribbon and proffers it to* JOE.)

NORMA

It's about Salome.
(MAX *arrives wheeling a silver trolley, with champagne, caviar and red Venetian glasses.* JOE *takes the manuscript from* NORMA *and settles himself.*)

NORMA

Salome: the story of a woman. The woman who was all women.

(He begins to read. MAX *withdraws.* NORMA *hovers,*
watching JOE.)

NORMA

 Salome, what a woman, what a part!
 Innocent body and a sinful heart,
 Inflaming Herod's lust,
 But secretly loving a holy man.
 No one could play her like I can.
 (She's off in a world of her own; so much so, that JOE *is*
 able to sing his lines directly to the audience, as he shifts
 through the pages and sips his champagne.)

JOE

 Well, I had nothing urgent coming up,
 I thought I might as well skim it.
 It's fun to see how bad bad writing can be,
 This promised to go to the limit.
 (NORMA *paces impatiently: the light is beginning to fade.)*

NORMA

 There's so many great scenes, I can't wait.
 A boiling cauldron of love and hate.
 She toys with Herod
 Till he's putty in her hands.
 He reels, tormented, through the desert sands.
 (MAX *reappears and moves around the room, lighting*
 lamps. JOE *picks up another bundle.)*

JOE

 It sure was a real cheery set-up,
 The wind wheezing through that organ.
 Max shuffling around and a dead ape dumped on a shelf.
 And her staring like a gorgon.
 (NORMA *is on the stairs now, peering across the room at*
 JOE.)*

NORMA

 They drag the baptist up from the jails.
 She dances the dance of the seven veils.

(NORMA *throws herself into an extravagant dance,
distracting* JOE.)

NORMA

Herod says: I'll give you anything.

(JOE *resumes reading as* MAX *shows in a man dressed in
formal evening clothes: the* PET UNDERTAKER. *He has a
baby coffin under his arm.*)

JOE

Now it was time for some comedy relief,
The guy with the baby casket.
Must have seen a thing or two, that chimp,
Shame it was too late to ask it.

(*During this,* MAX *and* NORMA *have followed the*
UNDERTAKER *out into the garden, he having stowed the
chimp in the coffin, wrapped in* NORMA's *shawl. Now*
NORMA *reappears suddenly, startling* JOE.)

NORMA

Have you got to the scene where she asks for his head?
If she can't have him living, she'll take him dead.
They bring in his head on a silver tray.
She kisses his mouth. It's a great screenplay!

(JOE's *on the last bundle now:* NORMA *lights herself a
Turkish cigarette, having first inserted it in a holder
attached to a curious clip which twists around her index
finger.*)

JOE

It got to be eleven, I was feeling ill.
What the hell was I doing?
Melodrama and sweet champagne
And a garbled plot from a scrambled brain;
But I had my own plot brewing.

(*He lays down the last page with a slight sigh.* NORMA *is
instantly alert.*)

JOE

Just how old is Salome?

27

(NORMA *doesn't bat an eyelid.*)

NORMA

Sixteen.

JOE

I see.

NORMA

Well?

JOE

It's fascinating.

NORMA

Of course it is.

(JOE *looks up at her, choosing his words judiciously.*)

JOE

Could be it's a little long,
Maybe the opening's wrong
But it's extremely good for a beginner.

NORMA

No, it's a perfect start,
I wrote that with my heart,
The river-bank, the baptist and the sinner.

JOE

Shouldn't there be some dialogue?

NORMA

I can say anything I want with my eyes.

JOE

It could use a few cuts.

NORMA

I will not have it butchered!

JOE

I'm not talking limb from limb,
I just mean a little trim.
All you need is someone who can edit.

NORMA

I want someone with a knack
Not just any studio hack

And don't think for a moment I'd share credit!
(NORMA *stares at him, an idea beginning to form in her mind.*)

NORMA

When were you born?

JOE

December twenty first, why?

NORMA

I like Sagittarians. You can trust them.

JOE

Thanks.
(*She turns on him, her eyes blazing.*)

NORMA

I want *you* to do this work.
(JOE *feigns a moment of surprise: then his eyes narrow and his voice is shrewd*.)

JOE

Me? I don't think I can. I'm busy. Just finished one script and about to start a new assignment.

NORMA

I don't care.

JOE

I'm pretty expensive. I get five hundred a week.

NORMA

Don't you worry about money. I'll make it worth your while.
(JOE *is still not giving anything away. He pretends to reflect.*)

JOE

Well. It's getting kind of late.

NORMA

Are you married, Mr . . . ?

JOE

The name is Gillis. Single.

NORMA
Where do you live?
JOE
Hollywood. Alto Nido Apartments.
NORMA
You'll stay here.
JOE
I'll come back early tomorrow.
NORMA
Nonsense, there's a room over the garage. Max will take you there. Max!
(*Rather unnervingly,* MAX *emerges from the shadows: he's been there for some time.*)
MAX
Yes, Madame.
NORMA
Take Mr Gillis to the guest room.
(*After a second's hesitation,* JOE *finds himself following* MAX *towards the French doors.*)
NORMA
We'll begin at nine sharp.

5: THE ROOM OVER THE GARAGE

MAX, *holding up a lamp, leads* JOE *across the dark patio and up an outside wooden staircase to a small, austere room above the garage, which* MAX *lights by screwing a light-bulb into the empty socket above the single bed.*

MAX
I made the bed up this afternoon.
JOE
Thanks.
(*He considers this for a moment.*)

JOE

How did you know I was going to stay?

MAX

There's soap and a toothbrush in the bathroom.

JOE

She's quite a character, isn't she, that Norma Desmond?
(MAX *is slightly scandalized by this remark; but he
preserves his dignity and looks* JOE *straight in the eye.*)

MAX

Once,
You won't remember,
If you said Hollywood, hers was the face you'd think of.
Her face
On every billboard,
In just a single week she'd get ten thousand letters.
Men would offer
Fortunes for a bloom from her corsage
Or a few strands from her hair.
Today
She's half-forgotten,
But it's the pictures that got small.
She is the greatest star of all.
Then,
You can't imagine,
The way fans sacrificed themselves to touch her shadow.
There was
A maharajah
Who hanged himself with one of her discarded stockings.
She's immortal,
Caught inside that flickering light beam
Is a youth which cannot fade.
Madame's
A living legend;
I've seen so many idols fall.
She is the greatest star of all.

(*He leaves the room.* JOE *watches him go, strangely*
impressed. Left alone, JOE *moves restlessly around the*
room for a moment.)

JOE

When he'd gone, I stood looking out of the window a
while. There was the ghost of a tennis court with faded
markings and a sagging net. There was an empty pool
where Clara Bow and Fatty Arbuckle must have swum ten
thousand midnights ago. And then there was something
else: the chimp's last rites, as if she were laying a child to
rest. Was her life really as empty as that?

(*As he speaks,* MAX *re-emerges below. He's carrying a*
shovel and, under his arm, the chimpanzee's coffin. He
advances to a spot where there's an overgrown rosebed in
the centre of the patio outside the French doors. As he
arrives there, NORMA, *who's evidently been waiting,*
emerges into the garden. They stand for a moment in silent
communion, the atmosphere solemn. Then MAX *takes up*
the shovel.

JOE *stands at the window, staring down at them, riveted by*
the peculiarity of the scene, shaking his head wonderingly.
Slow fade to black.)

6: SCHWAB'S DRUGSTORE

Schwab's is a Sunset Boulevard institution, a combination of
soda fountain, news-stand, tobacconist and diner: it's
crowded with movie people of one sort or another; including
some we recognize from the opening scene at Paramount,
MARY, *for example, whose day job is as a waitress at*
Schwab's (like Lana Turner); MYRON, *the director;* JOANNA,
the writer; and ARTIE GREEN. BETTY *sits in a booth, on her*
own, with her back to the door. A variety of conversations
and orders are in progress.

He says my screenplay's much too dark.
What do they know, those morons?
What's with you?
Some yes man
Just said no.
He asked me to screen test on my knees.
He's always been religious.
Who's your agent?
Marty Resnick.
Thought he went out of business.
Bring the check.
Ham on rye.
C'est la vie.
What are you playing?
Third policeman. (Cherry pie)
Wonderful great fantastic.
Where's your husband?
He's in Reno.
So are you free for dinner?
Time to go.
What's the rush? (Two large shakes)
Six broiled dogs
(*During this last round,* JOE *has entered the drugstore. He hesitates in the doorway, slightly disorientated by the hubbub and bustle after the sepulchral calm of* NORMA'S *house.* ARTIE *spots him and hurries over.*)

ARTIE
  Joe, you bastard, what brings you here?

JOE
  I'm taking a creative note
  From some snotty studio smart-ass.
  What's with you?

ARTIE
  I'm in love

JOE

What, again?

ARTIE

No, no, no.

This is it,

The real thing.

Never thought it could happen like this,

Saw myself as the Jewish Casanova,

But as soon as we shared our first kiss

I knew all my romancing days were over.

Now I'm up in the clouds and I'm head over heels.

I know it sounds corny,

But that's how it feels.

JOE

Great. Any chance of meeting this paragon.

ARTIE

Sure, just for a minute: she's due to have a meeting with some poor struggling hack.

(*He's steered* JOE *over to* BETTY's *booth: when she sees him, she rises to her feet.*)

BETTY

Hello, Mr Gillis.

ARTIE

You two know each other?

JOE

Yeah, I'm the hack.

ARTIE

Oh, I'm sorry. And she's the smart-ass?

BETTY

Just a minute, you're leaving me way behind here.

JOE

Don't worry, we'd better have our meeting, I don't want to come between you two lovebirds a minute longer than I have to. Oh, and congratulations. May I?

(He sits at the table next to BETTY, *pointing up at* ARTIE.)

JOE

He tells me you've made a new man of him.

(He turns to ARTIE.)

And you've done real well, I'd say. Of course, she could use a little guidance in the literary appreciation department.

BETTY

I like *Blind Windows*.

JOE

That's why I'm here.

BETTY

Have you had any ideas about how you could turn it into a movie?

*(*JOE *hesitates a moment; then settles back in his seat.)*

JOE

Girl meets boy.
That's a safe beginning.

ARTIE

Is this a western?
I love those wide rolling plains.

BETTY

No, it's not. They live in the city.

ARTIE

Then it's a thriller:
The sidewalk gleams when it rains.
Or how about a brilliant pianist?
Every time the full moon's on the rise
He can't play without a shot of virgin's blood.

BETTY

Thanks a lot.
Be sure to leave your number.

ARTIE

You'll think of something.
I'll see you opening night.

(*He moves off to join* MYRON *and* JOANNA *at another table.* BETTY *turns to* JOE.)

BETTY

Girl meets boy,
Now if I remember
She's a young teacher,
He's a reporter.
It's hate at first sight.

JOE

It won't sell,
These days they want glamour:
Fabulous heiress
Meets handsome Hollywood heel.
Problem is,
She thinks he's a dentist.
Would you believe it?
A wedding in the last reel.

BETTY

It doesn't have to be so mindless.
You should write from your experience
Give us something really moving; something true.

JOE

Who wants true?
Who the hell wants moving?
Moving means starving
And true means holes in your shoe.

BETTY

No, you're wrong.
They still make good pictures.
Stick to your story,
It's a good story.

JOE

OK, Miss Schaefer:
I give it to you.
(*He's on his feet;* BETTY *is looking up at him, completely*

36

wrong-footed by his unexpected reaction.)

BETTY

What do you mean?

JOE

What I say. It's all yours. I've given up writing myself. So
you write it.

BETTY

I'm not good enough to do it on my own. I thought we
could write it together.

JOE

I can't. I'm all tied up.

BETTY

Couldn't we work evenings? Six o'clock in the morning? I'll
come to your place.

JOE

Look, Betty, it can't be done. It's out.
(*He relents a little at her obvious disappointment, smiles
apologetically.*)

JOE

Let's keep in touch through Artie. That way if you get
stuck, we can consult. I've always been very liberal with
advice.
(*He smiles down at her, relaxed now.*)

JOE

Write this down,
I'll give you some ground rules.
Plenty of conflict
But nice guys don't break the law.
Girl meets boy,
Gives herself completely
And though she loves him,
She keeps one foot on the floor.

BETTY

No one dies except the best friend.
No one ever mentions communists.

37

No one takes a black friend to a restaurant.

JOE

Very good.
Nothing I can teach you.
We could have had fun
Fighting the studio.

BETTY

Yes, Mr Gillis,
That's just what I want.
(*They shake hands; the handshake lasts a little longer than is strictly necessary, is interrupted indeed by the arrival of* ARTIE.)

ARTIE

Not going, are you? Come to the movies with us.

JOE

No, I was just explaining to Betty, I've given up the movies.

ARTIE

Well, will we see you New Year's Eve, my place, same as ever?

JOE

Oh yes, sure, if you promise there'll be a lot of bad behaviour.

ARTIE

Guaranteed the worst in town.
(JOE *inclines his head to* BETTY.)

JOE

Miss Schaefer.

BETTY

Mr Gillis.

JOE

Good luck.
(*He turns and hurries out of the place.*)

*The house, ghostly in the moonlight. To begin with, the stage
is empty; then JOE appears, moving silently across the patio.
At a certain point he's startled, as MAX glides out through the
French doors to intercept him.*

MAX

Where have you been?

JOE

Out. I assume I can go out when I feel like it.

MAX

Madame is quite agitated. Earlier this evening, she wanted
you for something and you could not be found.

JOE

Well, that's tough.

MAX

I don't think you understand, Mr Gillis. Madame is
extremely fragile. She has moments of melancholy.

JOE

Why? Because of her career? She's done well enough. Look
at all the fan mail she gets every day.

MAX

I wouldn't look too closely at the postmarks if I were you.

JOE

You mean you send them?

MAX

Will you be requiring some supper this evening, sir?

JOE

No. And Max?

MAX

Yes, sir?

JOE

Who the hell do you think you are, bringing my stuff over
from my apartment without consulting me? I have a life of

my own: now you're telling me I'm supposed to be a
prisoner here?
(MAX *considers him for a moment, his eyes cold.*)
MAX
I think, sir, perhaps you will have to make up your mind to
abide by the rules of the house. That is if you want this job.
(*He turns: the house swallows him up and he disappears as
abruptly as he materialized.* JOE *stands for a moment,
perplexed: then he proceeds on his way up the wooden
staircase towards his room above the garage.*)

8: THE HOUSE ON SUNSET (INTERIOR)

A table has been cleared for JOE *in the main room. He sits at
the typewriter, the manuscript piled at his elbow, a pencil held
between his teeth, scissors and a pot of paste to hand.* NORMA
prowls the room, watching him avidly.

JOE
I started work on the script,
I hacked my way through the thicket,
A maze of fragmented ramblings
By a soul in limbo.
She hovered there like a hawk,
Afraid I'd damage her baby.
(JOE *drops a page of manuscript into the waste-paper
basket and* NORMA *reacts instantly.*)
NORMA
What's that?
JOE
I thought we might cut away from the slave market . . .
NORMA
Cut away from me?

JOE

They don't want you in every scene.

NORMA

Of course they do. What else would they have come for?
(*He sighs and retrieves the page. Presently, she leaves the room. Once she's gone,* JOE *drops the page back into the waste-paper basket and turns to the audience.*)

JOE

The house was always so quiet.
Just me and Max and the organ.
No one phoned and nobody ever came.
I couldn't breathe in that room
It was so full of Norma Desmond
And there was only one kind of entertainment on hand.
(*During this* MAX *has been busying himself, setting up a projector and lacing up the reels.* JOE *wanders over to take his place on the sofa. Eventually,* NORMA *sweeps in, dressed to the nines and settles down next to* JOE. MAX *switches on the projector and the beam radiates out across the auditorium. For a while, the whirr of the projector;* NORMA *watches, looking out into the audience, entranced; while* JOE, *far more detached, lights himself a cigarette, the smoke drifting across the light beam.*)

NORMA

This was dawn:
There were no rules,
We were so young.
Movies were born;
So many songs
Yet to be sung.
So many roads
Still unexplored;
We gave the world
New ways to dream.
Somehow we found

New ways to dream.
(*She takes* JOE's *arm excitedly and points up at the screen,*
somewhere above the audience's heads.)

NORMA

Joan of Arc:
Look at my face,
Isn't it strong?
There in the dark.
Up on the screen,
Where I belong.
We'll show them all
Nothing has changed.
We'll give the world
New ways to dream.
Everyone needs
New ways to dream.
(*By now, she's gripping on to* JOE, *who detaches himself*
gently and moves to the other end of the sofa, where he
turns to contemplate NORMA, *who's still staring*
ecstatically at the screen.)

JOE

I didn't argue,
Why hurt her?
You don't yell at a sleepwalker
Or she could fall and break her neck.
She smelled of faded roses.
It made me sad to watch her
As she relived her glory.
Poor Norma,
So happy,
Lost in her silver heaven.
(NORMA *continues to watch; and* JOE *watches her.*)

NORMA

They can't see where the future lies.
They don't recognize a star.

(JOE is touched; he reaches out and takes her hand.
Fade to black.)

9: THE HOUSE ON SUNSET

The sound of heavy rain. It's daytime but dull enough to need the lights on. JOE's typewriter is no longer on the table, but closed and standing on end on the floor. He's alone in the great room, playing solitaire. MAX is at the organ, wearing his white gloves, playing. JOE looks up at the audience, breaks off from his game.

JOE

In December, the rains came; right through the roof of my room above the garage. So she had me moved to the main house, to what Max called 'the room of the husbands'. On a clear day, the theory was, you could see Catalina. And little by little I worked through to the end of the script. At which point I might have left: only by then those two boys from the finance company had traced my car and towed it away.
(He resumes his game: all of a sudden NORMA sweeps out of her room and down the stairs; she's holding a fat typescript in her hand. She snaps at MAX.)

NORMA

Stop that!
(MAX stops playing.)
Well, today's the day.

JOE

What do you mean?

NORMA

Max is going to deliver the script to Paramount.

JOE

You're really going to give it to DeMille?

NORMA

I've just spoken to my astrologer. She read DeMille's horoscope: she read mine.

JOE

Did she read the script?

NORMA

DeMille is Leo; I'm Scorpio. Mars is transiting Jupiter and today is the day of closest conjunction.

JOE

Well, that's all right, then.

(NORMA *hands the typescript to* MAX.)

NORMA

Make sure it goes to Mr DeMille in person.

MAX

Very good, madame.

(*He leaves the house by the front door, having first put up an immense umbrella. There's a silence:* NORMA *moves up and down in a state of heightened emotion;* JOE *is steeling himself to broach a difficult subject.*)

JOE

Well . . .

NORMA

Great day.

JOE

It's been real interesting.

NORMA

Yes, hasn't it?

JOE

I want to thank you for trusting me with your baby.

NORMA

Not at all, it's I who should thank you.

JOE

Will you call and let me know as soon as you have some news?

(NORMA *frowns: she turns to him, with a bewildered expression.*)

NORMA

Call where?

JOE

My apartment.

NORMA

You can't possibly think of leaving now.

JOE

The script is finished, Norma.

NORMA

This is only the beginning, Joe, the first draft: I couldn't dream of letting you go, I need your support.

JOE

Well . . .

NORMA

You'll stay on full salary, of course . . .

JOE

It's not the money.

(NORMA *now has a look of genuine panic on her face: and* JOE *can see that some reassurance is essential.*)

JOE

Of course, I'll stay until we get some sort of a reaction from Paramount.

(*He's on his feet now; and* NORMA *grips his hand tightly for a moment.*)

NORMA

Thank you.

(*She releases his hand; and moves off leaving him a little shaken by this turn of events, his expression rueful. He turns to the audience.*)

JOE

Well, Max climbed into that old foreign bus in the garage, with its gold-plated speaking-tubes and leopard-skin upholstery and trundled down to Paramount to hand in our

masterpiece. And I settled down to wait for the inevitable
rejection.

10: THE HOUSE ON SUNSET

*A much brighter day: the shutters are open and the room is
flooded with light.* MAX *shows in an imposing, rather oily-
looking men's outfitter,* MR MANFRED, *who's followed by a
number of male assistants carrying armfuls of boxes and
teetering heaps of clothing. As they begin to deploy,* NORMA
bustles in from the patio.

NORMA

Hurry up, the birthday boy is on his way!
This is a surprise celebration.
I hope you've remembered everything I said,
I want to see a total transformation.
(JOE *wanders into the room: he stops in the doorway,
startled by the unaccustomed crowd.*)

JOE

What's all this?

NORMA

Happy Birthday, darling. Did you think we'd forgotten?

JOE

Well, I . . .

NORMA

These people are from the very best men's shop in town. I
had them close it down for the day.

JOE

But listen . . .

NORMA

Now I don't want to get under your feet, I'll leave you boys
to it.
(*And before* JOE *can stop her, she's gone again.* MANFRED

46

is already circling warily, trying to assess his new customer;
JOE *looks at him, obviously dismayed, a hint of rebellion in*
his expression.)

MANFRED

Happy Birthday, welcome to your shopathon!

JOE

What's going on?

MANFRED

Help yourself, it's all been taken care of.
Anyone who's anyone is dressed by me.

JOE

Well, golly gee.

MANFRED

Pick out anything you'd like a pair of.
You just point, I'll do the rest;
I've brought nothing but the best.
You're a very lucky writer.
Come along now, get undressed
Unless I'm much mistaken
That's a 42-inch chest.

JOE

I don't understand a word you're saying.

MANFRED

Well, all you need to know's the lady's paying.
It's nice to get your just reward this time of year.

JOE

Get outa here!

MANFRED

And all my merchandise is strictly kosher
When you've thrown away all your old worn-out stuff.

JOE

Hey, that's enough.

MANFRED

Perhaps you'd like to model for my brochure.
I have just the thing for you;

Chalk-stripe suits.

FIRST SALESMAN

    In black.

SECOND SALESMAN

       Or blue.

THIRD SALESMAN

  Glen plaid trousers.

FOURTH SALESMAN

    Cashmere sweaters.

FIFTH SALESMAN

  Bathing shorts for Malibu.

SIXTH SALESMAN

  Here's a patent leather lace-up.

SEVENTH SALESMAN

    It's a virtuoso shoe.

MANFRED

  And a simply marvellous coat made of vicuña.

JOE

  You know what you can do with your vicuña.
  (*At this delicate point,* NORMA *saunters back into the
  room. Oblivious to the atmosphere, she registers only that
  no progress has been made.*)

NORMA

  Come on, Joe, you haven't even started yet.

JOE

  You wanna bet?

NORMA

  I thought by now you'd look the height of fashion.
  (*She turns to* MANFRED.)

NORMA

  He always takes for ever making up his mind.
  (*And back to* JOE.)

NORMA

  Don't be unkind,
  I thought you writers knew about compassion.

48

(Impatient now, she plunges in among the clothes, towing
MANFRED *in her wake.)*

NORMA
 I love flannel on a man.
 (She picks out a beautiful pale jacket.)

MANFRED
 This will complement his tan.
 (Now she's grabbing at shirts and trousers.)

NORMA
 We'll take two of these and four of those.

MANFRED
 I'm still your greatest fan.
 (He turns back to JOE.)
 Very soon now we'll have stopped him
 Looking like an also-ran.

JOE
 You're going to make me sorry that I'm staying.

NORMA
 Well, all right, I'll choose, after all, I'm paying.
 (She picks out more and more clothes, handing them to the
 SALESMAN, JOE *slouching sullenly behind her.)*

MANFRED
 Evening clothes?

NORMA
                    I want to see your most deluxe.

JOE
 Won't wear a tux.

NORMA
 Of course not, dear, tuxedos are for waiters.

MANFRED
 What we need are tails, a white tie and top hat.

JOE
 I can't wear that.

NORMA
 Joe, second-rate clothes are for second-raters.

JOE

Norma, please . . .

NORMA

Shut up, I'm rich,
Not some platinum blonde bitch.
I own so many apartments
I've forgotten which is which.
I have oil wells in the desert.

(MANFRED *whispers to* JOE, *trying to make him see reason.*)

MANFRED

What a salesman, what a pitch!

(JOE *bridles: he grabs* MANFRED *by his exquisitely cut lapel.*)

JOE

I don't know what game you think you're playing.

(NORMA, *however, restrains him, with a heartfelt appeal.*)

NORMA

Joe, please don't spoil the fun I get from paying.

(*She disappears behind a portable clothes-rack and suddenly emerges with bowler hat and cane to give a dazzling Chaplin impression. Even* JOE *is charmed; and she finishes by taking a bow to general enthusiastic applause. Sensing her advantage now, she closes in on* JOE.)

NORMA

Joe, I'm sick to death of that
Same old filling-station shirt,
And that boring baggy jacket
Stained with yesterday's dessert.

JOE

I don't have to go to premières,
I'm never on display.
You seem to forget that I'm a writer,
Who cares what you wear when you're a writer?

(*But he's clearly weakening: and now* NORMA *moves in for the kill.*)

NORMA

I care, Joe, and please don't be so mean to me.

JOE

OK, all right.

NORMA

You'll be Prince Charming at my New Year's party.

JOE

I've been invited somewhere else on New Year's Eve.

NORMA

But that's our night.

JOE

I always see the New Year in with Artie.

NORMA

I can't do without you, Joe, I need you.

I've sent out every single invitation.

JOE

All right, Norma, I give in.

NORMA

Of course you do.

And when they've dressed you, you'll cause a sensation.
(*And with this she sweeps off, up the stairs.* JOE *and*
MANFRED *look at each other for a moment. Finally,* JOE
shrugs and spreads his arms, conceding. MANFRED *snaps
his fingers and the* SALESMEN *descend on* JOE, *engulfing
him, so that he disappears in the scrimmage.*)

SALESMEN

We equip the chosen few of Movieland.

MANFRED

(The latest cut.)

SALESMEN

We dress every movie star and crooner.

From their shiny toecaps to their hatband.

MANFRED

(Conceal your gut.)

You won't regret selecting the vicuña.

SALESMEN

If you need a hand to shake.
If there's a girl you want to make.
If there's a soul you're out to capture.
Or a heart you want to break.
If you want the world to love you.

MANFRED

You'll have to learn to take.
(*The* SALESMEN *move away from* JOE, *to reveal that he is now transformed, in full evening dress, white tie and tails.*)

SALESMEN

You must decide what part you are portraying.
(MANFRED *is now more or less cheek to cheek with* JOE. *He leans forward with offensive intimacy; the gloves are off.*)

MANFRED

And certain parts are worth the lady paying.

SALESMEN

And why not have it all? The lady's paying!
(*Blackout.*)

11: THE HOUSE ON SUNSET/
ARTIE GREEN'S APARTMENT

JOE *paces uneasily in his white tie and tails, as a Palm Court quartet begins playing tango music. He pauses to address the audience.*

JOE

I couldn't imagine what sort of a gallery of waxworks
Norma had invited to her New Year's Party: but she'd
certainly gone to town. I hadn't expected the place would
look like Times Square.
(*Lights up on the little orchestra, tucked in under the stairs:*

*the streamers, the trees in tubs, the floral arrangements, the
dozens of blazing candles.* MAX *appears with a glass in one
hand and a cocktail shaker in the other. He pours the
Martini and hands it to* JOE. *The silence between them is
somewhat oppressive until finally* JOE *breaks it when* MAX
returns with a tray of canapés.)

JOE

I suppose half the guests will be in wheelchairs, will they,
Max?

MAX

I couldn't tell you, sir. Madame made all the arrangements
herself.

(*Suddenly,* NORMA *appears at the top of the stairs in a
dazzling diamanté gown with long black gloves and bird of
paradise feathers in her hair. She begins a stately descent.*
JOE *puts his glass down and applauds.* MAX *watches
discreetly, evidently moved; he opens a bottle of
champagne.*

JOE *waits to meet her at the bottom of the stairs. He's
reaching out to take her arm, when as if from nowhere, she
suddenly produces a gold cigarette case and hands it to
him.*)

NORMA

Here. Happy New Year.

JOE

I can't take this, Norma.

NORMA

Shut up. Open it. Read what it says.

(JOE *opens it and reads out, half-amused and half-
appalled.*)

JOE

'Mad about the boy.'

NORMA

Yes; and you do look absolutely divine.

(JOE *is touched, despite his embarrassment; he decides to*

53

give in gracefully and slips the cigarette case into his pocket.)

JOE

Well, thank you.

(NORMA *stretches out a hand to lead* JOE *on to the freshly-waxed tiled dance floor.*)

NORMA

I had these tiles put in, you know, because Valentino said it takes tiles to tango. Come along.

JOE

Not on the same floor as Valentino!

NORMA

Just follow me.

(*They begin to dance. After a while,* NORMA *snaps at* JOE.)

NORMA

Don't lean back like that.

JOE

It's those feathers.

(NORMA *pulls the feathers out of her hair and casts them aside. They resume dancing, closer this time.*)

NORMA

Ring out the old,
Ring in the new;
A midnight wish
To share with you.
Your lips are warm,
My head is light;
Were we alive
Before tonight?
I don't need a crowded ballroom,
Everything I want is here.
If you're with me,
Next year will be
The perfect year.

(JOE *is becoming aware of what's happening; still, at the*

54

same time, he's caught up in the intoxication of the
moment.)

JOE

Before we play
Some dangerous game,
Before we fan
Some harmless flame,
We have to ask
If this is wise
And if the game
Is worth the prize.
With this wine and with this music,
How can anything be clear?
Let's wait and see,
It may just be
The perfect year.
(*They dance.*)

NORMA

It's New Year's Eve
And hopes are high,
Dance one year in,
Kiss one goodbye.
Another chance,
Another start,
So many dreams
To tease the heart.
We don't need a crowded ballroom,
Everything we want is here,
And face to face
We will embrace
The perfect year.
(*She kisses him lightly as the number comes to an end.*
Then, as the orchestra strikes up the next piece, they move
off the floor to take up the glasses of champagne which
MAX *has poured for them. They clink glasses and drink.*)

JOE

What time are they supposed to get here?

NORMA

Who?

JOE

The other guests.

NORMA

There are no other guests. Just you and me.
(*She leans in to kiss him again, this time more seriously.*
MAX *half turns away, averting his eyes.*)

NORMA

I'm in love with you. Surely you know that.
(JOE *is terribly startled by this; all he can do is begin to
bluster.*)

JOE

I'm all wrong for you, Norma; you need a big shot,
someone with polo ponies, a Valentino . . .

NORMA

What you're trying to say is that you don't want me to love
you. Is that it?
(JOE *doesn't answer: he looks away, avoiding her eye.
Thus, it takes him completely by surprise when she slaps his
face. And, before he can react, she's turned and run all the
way up the stairs to vanish into her bedroom.* JOE *finds
himself standing face to face with* MAX.)

JOE

Max.

MAX

Sir?

JOE

Get me a taxi.
(*As* MAX *moves towards the phone, the house moves back a
way to reveal* ARTIE's *apartment, a modest one-room
affair, packed to the rafters with carefree young people,
many of whom we have already encountered at the studio*

and at Schwab's. To one side of the stage, the microscopic bathroom is doing double duty as a dressing-room. Several of the GUESTS *cluster around the piano and there's a* GIRL *with a saxophone. Others help themselves to some dangerous looking alcoholic concoction from a punchbowl. The House at Sunset remains visible throughout. As the new scene establishes itself,* JOE *encases himself in his vicuña coat.*)

JOE

I had to get out.
I needed
To be with people my own age,
To hear the sound of laughter
And mix with hungry actors,
Underemployed composers,
Nicotine-poisoned writers,
Real people,
Real problems,
Having a really good time.
(JOE *hesitates in the doorway of the apartment, suddenly embarrassed by how overdressed he is. Meanwhile,* ARTIE *hails him and pushes through the crowd to greet him.*)

ARTIE

Gillis! We'd given up on you.
(BETTY, *by the piano, hears this and looks round, delighted to see* JOE. *By now,* ARTIE *has reached him.*)

ARTIE

Let me take your coat.
(*He touches the coat and reacts, surprised.*)

ARTIE

Jesus, Joe, what is this, mink?
(*He's even more surprised when the coat comes off to reveal Joe's tails.*)

ARTIE

Who did you borrow this from? Adolphe Menjou?

JOE
Close, but no cigar.
(*He gestures around the room.*)
Quite a crowd.

ARTIE
I invited all the kids doing walk-ons in *Samson and Delilah*.

BETTY
I'm glad you came. I want to talk to you.

JOE
Uh-oh.
(*Before she can develop this, an* ACTOR *starts the boys and girls off on their song.*)

ACTOR
You gotta say your New Year's resolution out loud.
(*He points, one by one, at a row of* ACTORS *on the sofa.*)

ACTRESS
By this time next year,
I'll have landed a juicy part.

SECOND ACTOR
Fifty-one's going to be my start.

THIRD ACTOR
No more carrying spears.

MARY
I'll be discovered,
My life won't ever be the same.
Billy Wilder will know my name
And he'll call all the time.

KATHERINE
Till he does can one of you guys
Lend her a dime?

SECOND ACTRESS
Just an apartment
With no roaches and no dry rot,

THIRD ACTRESS
Where the hot water comes out hot.

SECOND AND THIRD ACTRESSES
  That's my Hollywood dream.
JOANNA
  My resolution
  Is to write something that gets shot
  With approximately the plot
  I first had in my head.
MYRON
  But you'll get rewritten
  Even after you're dead.
ARTIE
  It's the year to begin a new life,
  Buy a place somewhere quiet, somewhere pretty.
  When you have a young kid and a wife
  Then you need somewhere green far from the city.
  It's a rambling old house with a big apple tree,
  With a swing for the kid and a hammock for me.
  (*The mood is broken, as a number of* GIRLS, *dressed as the*
  harem from Samson and Delilah *burst squealing out of the*
  bathroom followed by SAMMY, *wearing jodhpurs and*
  knee-length riding boots and carrying a megaphone. He
  adjusts his spectacles and assumes the grave, patriarchal air
  of CECIL B. DEMILLE.)
SAMMY
  Behold, my children,
  It is I, Cecil B. DeMille,
  Meeting me must be quite a thrill,
  But there's no need to kneel.
  I guarantee you
  Every girl in the chorus line
  Is a genuine Philistine.
  They don't come off the shelf,
  I flew every one in from Philistia myself.
  (*The girls dance a kind of parody Middle Eastern bump and*
  grind, at the end of which 'CECIL B' *raises the megaphone*

*to his lips and calls out: 'Lights! Cameras! Action!' At
which point a scantily clad 'SAMSON' rushes out of the
kitchen, his waist-length wig billowing out behind him,
pursued by a vampish 'DELILAH', brandishing a huge pair
of kitchen scissors. In the pandemonium, JOE has
gravitated towards BETTY.)*

GIRLS
This is the biggest film ever made!

SAMMY
Till my next project:
It's called *The Greatest Show on Earth*,
Three point six million dollars worth,
Lots of sawdust and sex.

(By now, JOE and BETTY are in the bathroom.)

JOE
How's your next project?

BETTY
Sheldrake's anxious to option it,
I've a feeling he smells a hit,
We've got so much to do.

JOE
Betty, you're forgetting, I gave it to you.

*(Two BOYS from the Samson company have begun a
ludicrous kind of sand dance with tea-towels as loincloths
and lampshades as fezzes.*
*Meanwhile, in the house, NORMA emerges from her room
and descends the stairs, walking carefully as if holding
herself together. MAX intercepts her with a glass of
champagne. She lights a cigarette, inserts it in her holder
contraption and begins pacing up and down, listening to
the orchestra with half an ear.*
*Back at Artie's apartment, when the dance is over, JOE sits
on the edge of the bath, contemplating BETTY.)*

JOE

> You remind me of me long ago,
> Off the bus, full of ignorant ambition.
> Thought I'd waltz into some studio
> And achieve overnight recognition.
> But an audience thinks when it's watching the screen,
> That the actors make up every word in the scene.
> (*At the house,* NORMA *drifts back upstairs with her glass of
> champagne.* MAX *watches her leave, very concerned.*
> ARTIE, *meanwhile, has wandered into the bathroom in
> search of* BETTY.)

BETTY

> I've done an outline,
> But I can't write it on my own.
> Can't we speak on the telephone?
> All my evenings are free.

ARTIE

> Hey, just a minute,
> I'm the fellow who bought the ring.

BETTY

> Artie, this is a business thing,
> It's important to me.
> You'll be on location in Clinch, Tennessee.
> (*She turns to* JOE, *talking with a real intensity.*)

BETTY

> Please make this your New Year's resolution for me.
> (*The* CHORUS *starts up again, out in the main room of the
> apartment.*)

ALL

> By this time next year,
> I will get my foot in the door.
> Next year I know I'm going to score
> An amazing success.
> Cut to the moment
> When they open the envelope,

Pass the statuette to Bob Hope
And it's my name you hear.
We'll be down on our knees
Outside Grauman's Chinese,
Palm prints there on the street,
Immortality's neat!
This time next year,
This time next year.
We'll have nothing to fear;
Contracts all signed,
Three-picture deal,
Yellow brick road career.
Hope we're not still saying these things
This time next year.
(*Back in the house,* MAX *is seized by a sudden fear. Moving with surprising speed, he suddenly bounds up the stairs and disappears into Norma's bedroom.*)

JOE

You know, I think I will be available in the New Year. In fact, I'm available right now.
(*He turns to* ARTIE:)
Where's your phone?

ARTIE

Down there. Of course, you'll have to move all my awards.

JOE

Listen, could you put me up for a couple of weeks?

ARTIE

It just so happens we have a vacancy on the couch.

JOE

I'll take it.
(*He pushes across to the phone, picks it up and dials. He has to put a finger in his ear, because some new piece of nonsense has started up in the room, a kind of spoof Apache dance.*
The phone rings in the house. It rings for some time; then

MAX *appears on the landing, where there's an extension, looking unprecedentedly ramshackle and dishevelled. He picks up the receiver.*)

MAX

Yes?

JOE

Max, this is Mr Gillis. I want you to do me a favour.

MAX

I cannot talk now, Mr Gillis.

JOE

Listen, I want you to get my old suitcase . . .

MAX

I'm sorry, I am attending to Madame.

JOE

What do you mean?

MAX

Madame found the razor in your room. And she cut her wrists.

(*Shock.* BETTY, *meanwhile, has been making her way over to speak to him. She arrives by his side and is immediately aware something is wrong.*)

BETTY

What's the matter?

(JOE *stares at her as if he's never seen her before in his life. Then, abruptly, he hangs up and, to* BETTY's *total astonishment, he pushes across the room, disrupting the cabaret, grabs his coat from the bookshelf where* ARTIE *has carefully stowed it, and slams out of the apartment.*

The apartment disappears; back in the house, the little orchestra is still playing to the empty room. Presently MAX *appears, supporting* NORMA. *Her wrists are heavily bandaged; she looks much older, frail and shaky. With infinite tenderness,* MAX *shepherds* NORMA *to the old sofa near the piano, out of sight of the orchestra. He's made the necessary preparations beforehand and now he drops to his*

knees and begins to bathe her forehead and temples with a
flannel dipped in iced water.
  Suddenly, JOE *bursts through the French doors, panting*
and extremely agitated. MAX *rises;* NORMA *half sits up,*
glaring at JOE.)

NORMA

Go away.

JOE

What kind of a silly thing was that to do?

NORMA

I'll do it again! I'll do it again! I'll do it again!

JOE

Attractive headline: GREAT STAR KILLS HERSELF FOR
UNKNOWN WRITER.

NORMA

Great stars have great pride.
(*She turns away from him.* MAX, *still anxious, is moving*
back, melting into the background.)

NORMA

You must have some girl; why don't you go to her?
(*Now* JOE *kneels beside* NORMA *and speaks to her with*
great gentleness.)

JOE

I never meant to hurt you, Norma. You've been good to
me. You're the only person in this stinking town that's ever
been good to me.

NORMA

Then why don't you say thank you and go? Go, go!
(JOE *leans forward and kisses her, as he does so, the*
orchestra segues into 'Auld Lang Syne'.)

JOE

Happy New Year.
(NORMA *reaches up and wraps her bandaged arms around*
his neck.)

NORMA
Happy New Year, darling.
(*They kiss again, a longer embrace. Then,* JOE *lifts her bodily, and carries her across the room. The orchestra plays on.* MAX *watches from the shadows, his expression grave and inscrutable, as* JOE *carries* NORMA *up the stairs. Through this, slow fade to black.*)

ACT TWO

12: THE HOUSE ON SUNSET

The exterior of the house in blazing sunshine. At first the stage is empty; and it remains so long enough to establish that the patio and garden have been tidied up and cut back. The pool has been cleaned and filled; and the visible portion of it ripples and sparkles.

Into this swims JOE, *swinging himself out of the pool in a single, supple movement. He sits for a moment, dangling his legs in the water, then reaches for a towel and gives himself a brief rub-down, before moving forward to address the audience.*

JOE
  Sure, I came out here
  To make my name,
  Wanted my pool, my dose of fame,
  Wanted my parking space at Warner's.
  But, after a year,
  A one-room hell,
  A Murphy bed,
  A rancid smell,
  Wallpaper peeling at the corners.
  Sunset Boulevard,
  Twisting Boulevard,
  Secretive and rich, a little scary.
  Sunset Boulevard,
  Tempting Boulevard,
  Waiting there to swallow the unwary.
  Dreams are not enough

To win a war,
Out here they're always keeping score
Beneath the tan the battle rages.
Smile a rented smile,
Fill someone's glass.
Kiss someone's wife,
Kiss someone's ass,
We do whatever pays the wages.
Sunset Boulevard,
Headline Boulevard,
Getting here is only the beginning.
Sunset Boulevard,
Jackpot Boulevard,
Once you've won you have to go on winning.
You think I've sold out?
Dead right I've sold out.
I've just been waiting
For the right offer:
Comfortable quarters,
Regular rations,
Twenty-four-hour
Five-star room service.
And if I'm honest,
I like the lady.
I can't help being
Touched by her folly.
I'm treading water,
Taking the money,
Watching her sunset . . .
Well, I'm a writer.
LA's changed a lot
Over the years,
Since those brave gold rush pioneers
Came in their creaky covered wagons.
Far as they could go,

End of the line.
Their dreams were yours,
Their dreams were mine.
But in those dreams
Were hidden dragons.
Sunset Boulevard,
Frenzied Boulevard,
Swamped with every kind of false emotion.
Sunset Boulevard,
Brutal Boulevard,
Just like you we'll wind up in the ocean.
She was sinking fast,
I threw a rope,
Now I have suits
And she has hope,
It seemed an elegant solution.
One day this must end,
It isn't real,
Still, I'll enjoy
A hearty meal
Before tomorrow's execution.
Sunset Boulevard,
Ruthless Boulevard,
Destination for the stony-hearted.
Sunset Boulevard,
Lethal Boulevard,
Everyone's forgotten how they started
Here on Sunset Boulevard.

(*He slips on a towelling robe and pours himself a glass of champagne from an open bottle. As he's sipping at it,* NORMA *comes hurrying out of the house in a state of high excitement.*)

NORMA
There's been a call,
What did I say?

They want to see
Me right away.
Joe, Paramount,
They love our child.
Mr DeMille
Is going wild.
(JOE *is a little surprised by this; but manages to conceal his*
scepticism almost at once.)

JOE

Well, that's wonderful, Norma.

NORMA

But it was some fool assistant,
Not acceptable at all.
If he wants me, then Cecil B.
Himself must call.
(JOE *shakes his head, a little disapproving.*)

JOE

I don't know if this is a time to stand on ceremony.

NORMA

I've been waiting twenty years now,
What's a few more days, my dear?
It's happened, Joe,
I told you so:
The perfect year.
(*She stretches out her hand to him, invitingly.*)

NORMA

Now let's go upstairs.

JOE

Don't you think you should at least call back?

NORMA

No: they can wait until I'm good and ready.
(*She leaves; and* JOE *turns to the audience.*)

JOE

It took her three days
And she was ready.

69

She checked with her astrologer,
Who sacrificed a chicken.
She dressed up like a pharaoh,
Slapped on a pound of make-up
And set forth in her chariot.
Poor Norma,
So happy,
Re-entering her kingdom.

13: ON THE ROAD

The Isotta-Fraschini moves in stately fashion down towards Hollywood.

MAX (*voice over*)
  If you will pardon me, Madame, the shadow over the left eye is not quite balanced.
NORMA (*voice over*)
  Thank you, Max.

14: PARAMOUNT

The shadow of the Isotta-Fraschini, as it pulls up outside the Paramount gates. MAX, *still offstage, blows the horn; at which, a young* STUDIO GUARD *breaks off the conversation he's been having with an* EXTRA *dressed as an Indian brave and walks over to confront* MAX, *as he enters.*

GUARD
  That's enough of that.
MAX
  We're here to see Mr DeMille. Open the gate.

GUARD

Mr DeMille is shooting. You need an appointment.

(*By now,* NORMA *and* JOE *have arrived onstage.*)

MAX

This is Norma Desmond. No appointment is necessary.

GUARD

Norma who?

(*Meanwhile, however,* NORMA *has recognised* JONES, *who's sitting on a wooden chair, reading a newspaper. She rolls down the window.*)

NORMA

Jonesy!

(JONES *looks up, frowning: then his expression clears.*)

JONES

Why, if it isn't Miss Desmond. How have you been, Miss Desmond?

NORMA

Fine, Jonesy. Open the gate.

(JONES *turns to his young colleague.*)

JONES

You heard Miss Desmond.

GUARD

They don't have a pass.

(JONES *shakes his head, exasperated; and opens the barrier himself. The car moves forward.*)

JONES

Stage 18, Miss Desmond.

NORMA

Thank you, Jonesy. And teach your friend some manners. Tell him without me there wouldn't be any Paramount Studio.

JONES

Get me Stage 18. I have a message for Mr DeMille.

(*As the car moves forward, crawling through the extras in costumes from the Westerns or war pictures or Roman epics,* JONES *picks up the phone. A scene-change reveals the cavernous interior of Sound Stage 18, where the stand-ins for Victor Mature and Hedy Lamarr are in position, in a blaze of light, on the grandiose* Samson and Delilah *set. Mr DeMille, recognisable from the parody version of Act I, confers with his director of photography. He's interrupted by one of his assistants,* HEATHER, *who approaches with some trepidation.*)

HEATHER
Mr DeMille.

DEMILLE
What is it?

HEATHER
Norma Desmond is here to see you.

DEMILLE
Norma Desmond?

HEATHER
She's right here at the studio.

DEMILLE
It must be about that appalling script of hers. What shall I say?

HEATHER
I could give her the brush.
(*He turns back towards the set.*)

DEMILLE
Thirty million fans have given her the brush. Isn't that enough? I'll be back in a minute.
(*He disappears into the recesses of the studio as* NORMA *arrives outside with* MAX *and* JOE. *The shadow of the Isotta is thrown against the wall of the studio.* NORMA *hesitates for a moment, gripping* JOE's *hand fiercely.*)

NORMA
Won't you come along, darling?
(JOE *shakes his head.*)

JOE

It's your script. It's your show. Good luck.

NORMA

Thank you, darling.

(*By this time,* HEATHER *has emerged from the studio. She comes over to greet* NORMA.)

HEATHER

This way, Miss Desmond.

(DEMILLE *steps out to greet her; he envelops her in his arms.*)

DEMILLE

Well, well, well.

NORMA

Hello, Mr DeMille.

(*A long embrace.*)

NORMA

Last time I saw you was someplace terribly gay. I was dancing on a table.

DEMILLE

A lot of people were. Lindbergh had just landed.

(*He starts to lead her into the studio.*)

NORMA

You read the script, of course.

DEMILLE

Well, yes . . .

NORMA

I know how busy you are when you're shooting, but I do think you could have picked up the phone yourself, instead of leaving it to some assistant.

DEMILLE

I don't know what you mean, Norma.

NORMA

Oh, yes you do.

DEMILLE

Come on in.

(*He leads her into the studio; a bewildering chaos of activity, which at first stuns her. He shouts to be heard above the cacophony.*)

DEMILLE

Sit over there in my chair, Norma, I have to finish my camera rehearsal.

(*He hurries off. Slowly, as* NORMA *looks around, the sound fades to nothing. She stands there, gradually coming to terms with the old familiar space. Suddenly, a* VOICE *rings out.*)

VOICE

Miss Desmond! Hey, Miss Desmond!

(NORMA *looks around, unable to identify the source of the* VOICE.)

VOICE

Up here, Miss Desmond: it's Hog-eye!

(NORMA *looks up: up in the flies, balanced on the walkway, is a quite elderly electrician.*)

NORMA

Hog-eye! Well, hello!

HOG-EYE

Let's get a look at you.

(*And so saying, he swivels one of the big lamps until it finds her. She stands for a moment, isolated, bathed in light. Then, murmuring among themselves, from all over the studio, technicians, extras and stagehands, begin to converge on her.*)

NORMA

I don't know why I'm frightened,
I know my way around here:
The cardboard trees,
The painted seas,
The sound here.
Yes, a world to rediscover
But I'm not in any hurry

And I need a moment.
The whispered conversations
In overcrowded hallways,
The atmosphere
As thrilling here
As always.
Feel the early morning madness,
Feel the magic in the making,
Why, everything's as if we never said goodbye.
I've spent so many mornings
Just trying to resist you.
I'm trembling now
You can't know how
I've missed you,
Missed the fairy-tale adventures
In this ever-spinning playground,
We were young together.
I'm coming out of make-up,
The lights already burning.
Not long until
The cameras will
Start turning
And the early morning madness
And the magic in the making.
Yes, everything's as if we never said goodbye.
I don't want to be alone;
That's all in the past.
This world's waited long enough
I've come home at last.
And this time will be bigger
And brighter than we knew it,
So watch me fly,
We all know I
Can do it.
Could I stop my hand from shaking?

Has there ever been a moment
With so much to live for?
The whispered conversations
In overcrowded hallways,
So much to say,
Not just today,
But always.
We'll have early morning madness,
We'll have magic in the making,
Yes, everything's as if we never said goodbye.
(*The studio staff bursts into spontaneous applause and*
DEMILLE, *moved, cradles* NORMA *in his arms.*

The focus shifts to outside the studio, where JOE *has
moved off to lean against a wall, smoke a cigarette and
enjoy the passing parade. Suddenly he sees* BETTY *hurrying
past, a bundle of scripts under her arm. He grinds out his
cigarette and steps forward to intercept her, surprising her
considerably.*)

JOE
  Hi there, Betty.
BETTY
  What are you doing?
JOE
  I'm out here for a meeting.
BETTY
  Where have you been keeping yourself?
JOE
  Someone's been doing it for me.
BETTY
  We should talk.
JOE
  Gotta run.
BETTY
  Hold it, Joe.
  I can't write this

On my own,
I thought you said you'd help me.

JOE

I'm real sorry,
New Year's crisis,
Would you believe a sick friend?
It's just not
A good time.
Not right now.

BETTY

Well, when is a good time?

JOE

I will call you, I promise.
(BETTY *looks at him for a moment.*)

BETTY

I guess I'll have to trust you.

JOE

Thanks. I won't let you down.
(BETTY *smiles at him and hurries on.*
During all this, MAX *has been attending to some imaginary*
speck on the mudguard of the Isotta. This enables him
deliberately to ignore SHELDRAKE, *who has emerged from*
the studio and has been trying to catch his attention.
Eventually, he straightens up and turns to him, his
eyebrows raised interrogatively.)

SHELDRAKE

Don't you work for Norma Desmond? A couple of weeks
ago, I'm looking out of my office window and I saw you
driving on to the lot. And I said that's exactly the car I've
been looking for. Great for my Crosby picture. So I made
some enquiries and I've been calling for two weeks. Doesn't
she ever answer the phone?

MAX

Go away.

SHELDRAKE

It's so perfect, you can't find that kind of thing outside of a
museum. And we'll pay. I plan to offer her . . . a hundred
dollars a week.

MAX

Go away: and don't you dare speak to her.

SHELDRAKE

What are you crazy?
(MAX *shoos him away.*
In the studio, DEMILLE *has been attempting to set up his
shot. Now, however, unable to ignore the kerfuffle
surrounding* NORMA, *he steps down and approaches her;*
NORMA *turns to him, radiant.*)

NORMA

Did you see
How they all came
Crowding around?
They still love me
And soon we'll be
Breaking new ground.
Brave pioneers.

DEMILLE

Those were the days.

NORMA

Just like before.

DEMILLE

We had such fun.

NORMA

We'll give the world
New ways to dream.
Norma and DeMille
We always found
New ways to dream.
(*The red light goes on and the studio bell shrills.* VICTOR
MATURE *and* HEDY LAMARR *arrive to take the place of*

78

their identically costumed stand-ins.)

DEMILLE

Let's have a good long talk one day.

NORMA

The old team will be back in business.

DEMILLE

Sorry, my next shot's ready.
(*He begins to walk her towards the studio door.
Meanwhile, outside, JOE has moved over towards MAX and
notices right away, from the latter's thunderous expression,
that something disturbing has happened.*)

JOE

What's the matter, Max?

MAX

I just found out the reason for all those phone calls from
Paramount.

JOE

Yes?

MAX

It's not Madame they want. It's her car.

JOE

Oh, my God.
(*DEMILLE and NORMA have reached the doorway of the
studio.*)

NORMA

Now, you remember, don't you? I don't work before ten or
after four-thirty in the afternoon.

DEMILLE

It isn't entirely my decision, Norma, New York must be
consulted.

NORMA

That's fine. You ask any exhibitor in the country. I'm not
forgotten.

DEMILLE

Of course you're not.

(*He embraces her.*)

DEMILLE

Goodbye, young fellow. We'll see what we can do.

NORMA

I'm not worried. It's so wonderful to be back.
(*She turns and sweeps into the car, the door of which* MAX *is already holding open.* DEMILLE *waves goodbye to her; then, as the Isotta drives off, he shakes his head, disturbed, and moves, preoccupied, back into the studio.* HEATHER *is waiting for him and* BETTY *is also among the milling crowd.*)

BETTY

Was that really Norma Desmond?

DEMILLE

It was.

HEATHER

She must be about a million years old.

DEMILLE

I hate to think where that puts me. I could be her father.

HEATHER

I'm sorry, Mr DeMille.
(*The shot is ready; and everyone is waiting on* DEMILLE'*s orders: but he pauses for a moment, in pensive mood, his hand on the back of his chair.*)

DEMILLE

If you could have seen
Her at seventeen
When all of her dreams were new,
Beautiful and strong,
Before it all went wrong:
She's never known the meaning of surrender;
Never known the meaning of surrender.
(*Slow fade to black.*)

Night on the Paramount lot. Betty's office is a spartan affair, one of a row of wooden cubicles suspended at first floor level, above the darkened streets of the back lot. BETTY *sits behind her desk, staring at her typewriter, from which a piece of paper protrudes;* JOE, *in his shirtsleeves, paces up and down, holding a pencil. Presently, as the silence extends, he crosses to look down at the sheet of paper in his typewriter, frowns; then, his brow clears as an idea occurs to him.*

JOE

    How about
    They don't know each other;
    He works the night shift
    And she takes classes all day?
    Here's the thing,
    They both share the same room,
    Sleep in the same bed;
    It works out cheaper that way.

BETTY

    Well, I've a feeling you're just kidding
    But to me it sounds believable;
    Makes a better opening than that car chase scene.
    Girl finds boy,
    Borrowing her toothbrush
    Or oversleeping
    Or at her sewing-machine.
    (*She's got up as the excitement over her ideas has gripped her; and now* JOE *takes her place behind the typewriter.*)

JOE

    It's not bad, there are some real possibilities . . .
    (BETTY *picks up Joe's cigarette case, helps herself to a cigarette and then notices the inscription.*)

BETTY

Who's Norma?

JOE

Who's who?

BETTY

I'm sorry, I don't usually read private cigarette cases.

JOE

Oh, well, Norma's a friend of mine, middle-aged lady, very foolish, very generous.

BETTY

I'll say: this is solid gold. 'Mad about the boy'?

(JOE *rises to his feet, thinks of a way to change the subject*.)

JOE

How's Artie?

BETTY

Stuck in Tennessee. It rains all the time, they're weeks behind. Nobody knows when they'll get back.

JOE

Good.

BETTY

What's good about it? I'm missing him something fierce.

JOE

No, I mean this idea we had is really pretty good.

(*He picks up the notebook, scribbles a note, as* BETTY *moves back towards the desk*.)

JOE

Back to work.

BETTY

What if *he's* a teacher?

JOE

Where does that get us?
Don't see what good it would do.

BETTY

No, its great,
If they do the same job . . .

JOE
    So much in common.
    They fall in love, wouldn't you?
    (*Now* BETTY *is thinking better of her idea.*)
BETTY
    Ah, yes, but if he's just a teacher,
    We lose those scenes in the factory.
JOE
    Not if he's a champion for the working man.
    Girl likes boy,
    She respects his talent.
BETTY
    Working with someone
    Can turn you into a fan.
JOE
    This is fun,
    Writing with a partner.
BETTY
    Yes, and it could be . . .
JOE
    Helluva movie.
BETTY
    Can we really do this?
JOE AND BETTY
    I know that we can!
    (*Blackout.*)

16: THE HOUSE ON SUNSET

The drawing-room, gloomy and cavernous as ever. JOE *sits under one of the lamps, reading a book.* NORMA, *her face invisible, lies face-down on the massage table, covered only by a towel, surrounded by women. A* MASSEUSE *is working on her legs; an immaculate* BEAUTICIAN, *a blonde, is attending*

83

to her cuticles; a woman ASTROLOGER *in a headscarf hovers about the top end of the table; and several others hover around.*

ASTROLOGER

I don't think you should shoot before July 15th.
Right now is a perilous time for Pisces.
If you wait till Venus is in Capricorn
You'll avoid a catalogue of crises.
(*The* MASSEUSE *drums away at her thighs.*)

MASSEUSE

I need three more weeks to get these thighs in shape.
No more carbohydrates, don't be naughty,

SECOND MASSEUSE

We'll soon have you skipping like an *ingénue*
You won't look a day over forty.
(*At this point,* NORMA *turns her face to look downstage and we see that it's coated in some thick white gunk, with slices of cucumber covering her eyes. Meanwhile,* JOE *puts his book down, checks his watch, gets up and begins moving round the room, trying to appear casual, but evidently looking for something.*)

BEAUTICIAN

We have dry heat, we have steam,
We have moisturising cream.
We have mud-packs, we have blood-sacks,
It's a rigorous regime.
Not a wrinkle when you twinkle
Or a wobble when you walk,
Of course, there's bound to be a little suffering;
Eternal youth is worth a little suffering.

ANALYST

Listen to your superego not your id;
Age is just another damn neurosis,
I'll have you regressing back to infancy

84

And back into the womb under hypnosis.

DOCTOR

I inject the tissue of the foetal lamb;
The formula's the one Somerset Maugham owns.
Just a modest course of thirty-seven shots
And you will be a heaving mass of hormones.

ALL

No more crow's feet, no more flab,
No more love handles to grab.
You'll be so thin they'll all think you're
Walking sideways like a crab.
Nothing sagging, nothing bagging,
Nothing dragging on the floor.
Of course, there's bound to be a little suffering
Eternal youth is worth a little suffering.

(*With this the beauty team packs up and leaves, shown out by* MAX. JOE, *still looking, winds up in* NORMA's *vicinity. She suddenly produces a script from under a towel.*)

NORMA

Is this what you're looking for, by any chance?

JOE

Why, yes.

NORMA

Whose phone number is this?

(JOE *takes the script from her, very sheepish, not answering.* NORMA *rises from the massage table, gathering her towel about her, peeling the cucumber slices from her eyes.*)

NORMA

I've been worried about the line of my throat. This woman has done wonders with it.

JOE

Good.

NORMA

And I've lost half a pound since Tuesday.

JOE

Very good.

NORMA

And now it's after nine. I'd better get to bed.

JOE

You had.

NORMA

Are you coming up?

JOE

I think I'll read a little longer.

NORMA

You went out last night, didn't you, Joe?

JOE

I went for a walk.

NORMA

You took the car.

JOE

I drove to the beach.

NORMA

Who's Betty Schaefer?
(*Silence. Eventually,* JOE *shakes his head.*)

JOE

Surely you don't want me to feel I'm a prisoner in this house?

NORMA

You don't understand, Joe, I'm under such a terrible strain. It's been so hard I even got myself a revolver. The only thing that stopped me using it was the thought of all those people waiting to see me back on the screen. How could I disappoint them? So all I ask is a little patience, a little understanding.

JOE

Norma, there's nothing to worry about, I haven't done anything.

NORMA

Of course you haven't. Good night, my darling.
(*She kisses him lightly, as best she can in the circumstances, and sets off upstairs, a bizarre figure in her mask and white towel.* JOE *waits until she's disappeared and gathers up his script. Then he turns to the audience.*)

JOE

I should have stayed there.
Poor Norma,
So desperate to be ready
For what would never happen.
But Betty would be waiting,
We had the script to finish:
One unexpected love scene
Two people
Both risking
A kind of happy ending.
(*He slips quietly out through the French doors. As he does so,* MAX, *previously seen escorting the beauty team out, quite unexpectedly emerges from the shadows of some recess in the room. His expression is troubled. Fade to black.*)

17: BETTY'S OFFICE
AND THE BACK LOT AT PARAMOUNT

It's night again on the Paramount lot and BETTY *is once again at her typewriter: but this time there's some light on the standing New York street set, which is being dressed for action the following day.* JOE *watches as* BETTY *finishes typing.*

BETTY

T-H-E-E-N-D! I can't believe it, I've finished my first script!

JOE

Stop it, you're making me feel old.

BETTY

It's exciting, though, isn't it?

JOE

How old are you, anyway?

BETTY

Twenty-two.

JOE

Smart girl.

BETTY

Shouldn't we open some champagne?

JOE

Best I can offer is a stroll to the water cooler at the end of
the lot.

BETTY

Sounds good to me. I love the back lot here. All cardboard,
all hollow, all phoney, all done with mirrors; I think I love
it better than any street in the world. I spent my childhood
here.

JOE

What were you, a child actress?

BETTY

No, but my family always expected me to become a great
star. I had ten years of dramatic lessons, diction, dancing,
everything you can think of: then the studio made a test.

JOE

That's the saddest story I ever heard.

BETTY

I was born two blocks from here. My father was head
electrician at the studio until he died, and mother still
works in wardrobe.

JOE

Second generation, huh?

88

BETTY
  Third. Grandma did stunt work for Pearl White.
  (*As they walk down the Manhattan street, the stage begins
  to revolve slowly, so that they end up walking downstage;
  and the flimsy struts holding up the substantial sets are
  gradually revealed.*
  JOE *and* BETTY *walk in silence for a while;* BETTY's
  *expression is deeply preoccupied. They come to a halt in
  front of the water cooler.*)
JOE
  I guess it is kind of exciting, at that, finishing a script.
  (*He fixes a couple of paper cups of water; and hands one to*
  BETTY, *who's miles away and comes to with a start when
  he touches her arm.*)
BETTY
  What?
JOE
  Are you all right?
BETTY
  Sure.
JOE
  Something's the matter, isn't it?
  (*Pause. Then* BETTY *blurts out.*)
BETTY
  I had a telegram from Artie.
JOE
  Is something wrong?
BETTY
  He wants me to come out to Tennessee. He says it would
  only cost two dollars to get married in Clinch.
JOE
  Well, what's stopping you? Now we've finished the
  script . . .
  (*He breaks off, amazed to see that she's crying.*)

JOE

Why are you crying? You're getting married, isn't that what
you wanted?

BETTY

Not any more.

JOE

Don't you love Artie?

BETTY

Of course I do. I'm just not in love with him any more,
that's all.

JOE

Why not? What happened?

BETTY

You did.

(*Suddenly, they're in each other's arms. A long kiss.*)

BETTY

When I was a kid,
I played on this street,
I always loved illusion.
I thought make-believe
Was truer than life
But now it's all confusion.
Please can you tell me what's happening?
I just don't know any more.
If this is real,
How should I feel?
What should I look for?

JOE

If you were smart,
You would keep on walking
Out of my life
As fast as you can.
I'm not the one
You should pin your hopes on,
You're falling for

The wrong kind of man.
This is crazy.
You know we should call it a day.
Sound advice, great advice,
Let's throw it away.
I can't control
All the things I'm feeling,
I haven't got a prayer.
If I'm a fool, well, I'm too much in love to care.
I knew where I was,
I'd given up hope,
Made friends with disillusion.
No one in my life,
But I look at you
And now it's all confusion.

BETTY

Please can you tell me what's happening?
I just don't know any more.
If this is real,
How should I feel?
What should I look for?
I thought I had
Everything I needed.
My life was set,
My dreams were in place.
My heart could see
Way into the future.
All of that goes
When I see your face.
I should hate you,
There I was, the world in my hand
Can one kiss kiss away
Everything I planned?
I can't control
All the things I'm feeling,

I'm floating in mid-air.
I know it's wrong, but I'm too much in love to care.
BETTY AND JOE
I thought I had
Everything I needed.
My life was set,
My dreams were in place.
My heart could see
Way into the future.
All of that goes
When I see your face.
This is crazy.
You know we should call it a day.
Sound advice, great advice,
Let's throw it away.
I can't control
All the things I'm feeling,
We're floating in mid-air.
If we are fools, well, we're too much in love to care.
If we are fools, well, we're too much in love to care!
(*By now, they're halfway up the stairs on their way back to the office. They fall into each other's arms and embrace passionately. Then* JOE *leads* BETTY *by the hand back into the office. They kiss again and it's obvious that they're about to make love.* JOE's *hand reaches out to turn off the light in the office.*)

18: THE HOUSE ON SUNSET (EXTERIOR)

It's late at night as JOE, *in the Isotta, glides back into the garage. He steps down from the car with a gleam in his eye and a spring in his step; and is therefore thoroughly startled when the sombre figure of* MAX *steps forward out of the darkness. However, he recovers quickly. It's a murky night, wind rising, rain threatening.*

JOE

What is it, Max? You waiting to wash the car?

MAX

Please be very careful as you cross the patio. Madame may be watching.

JOE

Suppose I tiptoe up the back stairs and undress in the dark, will that do it?

MAX

It's just that I am greatly worried about Madame.

JOE

Well, we're not helping any, feeding her lies and more lies. What happens when she finds out they're not going to make her picture?

MAX

She never will. That is my job. I made her a star and I will never let her be destroyed.

JOE

You made her a star?

MAX

I directed all her early pictures. In those days there were three young directors who showed promise: D. W. Griffith, Erich von Stroheim and . . .
(JOE *interrupts, as the realisation suddenly dawns on him.*)

JOE

You must be Max Mayerling.

MAX

That's right.
(*By now, they've moved out of the garage on to the dimly lit patio.*)

MAX

    When we met
    She was a child,
    Barely sixteen;
    Awkward and yet
    She had an air
    I'd never seen.
    I knew I'd found
    My perfect face.
    Deep in her eyes,
    New ways to dream,
    And we inspired
    New ways to dream.
    Talkies came:
    I stayed with her,
    Took up this life,
    Threw away fame.
    (*He hesitates, before steeling himself to go on.*)
    Please understand,
    (*A beat.*)
    She was my wife.
    (*Pause.* JOE *is staggered.* MAX *is fighting back a wave of emotion.*)
    We had achieved
    Far more than most.
    We gave the world
    New ways to dream.
    Everyone needs
    New ways to dream.
    (JOE *shakes his head, still incredulous.*)

JOE

    You're telling me you were married to her?

MAX

    I was the first husband.

NORMA, *her face now bare of make-up, wearing a white negligée, her expression profoundly tormented, picks up the phone and dials.*

NORMA

Hello, is this Gladstone 9281? Miss Schaefer? . . . Miss Schaefer, you must forgive me for calling so late, but I really feel it's my duty. It's about Mr Gillis . . . You do know a Mr Gillis? Well, exactly how much do you know about him? Do you know where he lives? Do you know what he lives on? (*At around this point,* JOE, *unseen by* NORMA, *steps in through the French doors and freezes in the shadows, listening.*)

NORMA

I want to spare you
A lot of sadness.
I don't know what he's told you,
But I can guarantee you
He doesn't live with mother
Or what you'd call a room-mate.
He's just a . . . I can't say it.
Poor Betty
You ask him,
I'd love to hear his answer.
(*She's completely taken by surprise, as* JOE *snatches the receiver from her.*)

JOE

That's right, Betty, why don't you ask me? Or better yet, come over and see for yourself. Yes, right now. The address is ten thousand eighty six, Sunset Boulevard. (*He hangs up violently and turns to stare at* NORMA *in furious silence. She flinches under his gaze.*)

NORMA

Don't hate me, Joe. I did it because I need you. Look at me.

Look at my hands. Look at my face. Look under my eyes.
How can I go back to work if I'm wasting away?
(JOE *says nothing: he's trying to control his rage.*)

NORMA

Don't stand there hating me. Shout at me, strike me, but
don't hate me.
(*But* JOE, *who has been looking at her with an expression
of infinite contempt, deliberately turns his back on her.
A distant rumble of thunder: and an orchestral* INTERLUDE
*begins, during which the storm intensifies, a torrential
tropical rain starts to fall, lightning flashes and* NORMA
makes her way shakily up the stairs. JOE *paces, steeling
himself for the coming encounter.* NORMA *vanishes into her
bedroom,* JOE *finally slumps on the big sofa. Unseen by
him,* NORMA *re-emerges, quietly, on to the landing: she's
holding a revolver. She sinks to the floor and waits.
The shrill of the doorbell.* JOE *springs to his feet and
hurries to let* BETTY *in.*)

JOE

Come on in.
(*He leads* BETTY *into the main room. She looks round for a
moment, unnerved by the size of the place.*)

BETTY

What's going on, Joe?
Why am I so scared?
What was that woman saying?
She sounded so weird,
I don't understand . . .
Please can't you tell me what's happening?
Don't you love me any more?
Shall I just go?
Say something, Joe.
(NORMA *moves stealthily forward, staring down at* BETTY
through the balustrade.)

JOE
Have some pink champagne
And caviar,
When you go visit with a star,
The hospitality is stellar.
BETTY
So this is where you're living.
JOE
Yes, it's quite a place:
Sleeps seventeen,
Eight sunken tubs,
A movie screen,
A bowling alley in the cellar.
BETTY
I didn't come to see a house, Joe.
JOE
Sunset Boulevard,
Cruise the Boulevard,
Win yourself a Hollywood palazzo.
Sunset Boulevard,
Mythic Boulevard,
Valentino danced on the terrazzo.
BETTY
Who's it belong to?
JOE
Just look around you.
BETTY
That's Norma Desmond.
(*She's seen the big portrait above the fireplace; now* JOE
*begins to draw her attention to some of the innumerable
other portraits, photographs and stills.*)
JOE
Right on the money.
That's Norma Desmond,
That's Norma Desmond,

That's Norma Desmond.

That's Norma Desmond.

BETTY

Why did she call me?

JOE

Give you three guesses.
It's the oldest story
In the book:
Come see the taker being took.
The world is full of Joes and Normas.
Older woman,
Very well-to-do,
Meets younger man.
A standard cue
For two mechanical performers.

(BETTY *puts a hand over his mouth*.)

BETTY

Just pack your things and let's get out of here.

JOE

You mean *all* my things?
Have you gone mad?
Leave all the things I've never had?
Leave this luxurious existence?
You want me to face
That one-room hell,
That Murphy bed,
That rancid smell,
Go back to living on subsistence?
It's no time to begin a new life,
Now I've finally made a perfect landing.
I'm afraid there's no room for a wife,
Not unless she's uniquely understanding.
You should go back to Artie and marry the fool
And you'll always be welcome to swim in my pool.

BETTY

I can't look at you any more, Joe.
(*She turns and rushes blindly out of the French door,
leaving it open. Wind and rain.* JOE's *head slowly sinks;
he's overcome by a wave of misery. Meanwhile, on the
landing,* NORMA *scrambles to her feet. The revolver is no
longer in evidence. She crosses the landing and starts off
down the stairs: a flutter of movement catches* JOE's *eye
and he turns.* NORMA *stops on the stairs, temporarily
halted by the fierceness of his expression, but as he moves
towards her and starts up the stairs, she stretches out a
hand to him.*)

NORMA

Thank you, thank you, Joe, thank you.
(JOE *brushes past her, brusquely shaking off her hand as
she touches his wrist and vanishes into his room. She stays
where she is, uncertain, unable to make sense of what's
happening; and, suddenly,* JOE *reappears. He's carrying his
battered old typewriter. Calm and unhurried, he starts off
down the stairs again, as* NORMA *stares wildly at him.*)

NORMA

What are you doing, Joe?
(*He ignores her, continues to move evenly down the stairs.*)

NORMA

You're not leaving me?

JOE

Yes, I am, Norma.

NORMA

You can't! Max! Max!

JOE

**It's been a bundle of laughs
And thanks for the use of the trinkets.**
(*He takes the gold cigarette case out of his pocket and
hands it to her.*)

JOE

A little ritzy for the copy desk
Back in Dayton.
(*He starts to move on, then turns back to her, his
expression serious.*)
And there's something you ought to know.
I want to do you this favour:
They'll never shoot that hopeless script of yours.
They only wanted your car.
(*During this,* MAX *has entered, below. He looks on,
helpless.*)

NORMA

That's a lie! They still want *me*!
What about all my fan mail?

JOE

It's Max who writes you letters.
Your audience has vanished.
They left when you weren't looking.
Nothing's wrong with being fifty
Unless you're acting twenty.
(*He sets off down the stairs.*)

NORMA

I am the greatest star of them all.

JOE

Goodbye, Norma.
(*He's spoken without looking back; so he doesn't see*
NORMA *fetch the revolver out of her pocket and point it at
him.*)

NORMA

No one ever leaves a star.
(*She fires.* JOE *looks extremely surprised, but carries on
walking, for the moment apparently unaffected. At the
bottom of the stairs, he lets go of the typewriter, which
crashes down on to the tiles. He staggers slightly, but
carries on, out through the French door.* NORMA *hurries*

*after him. Outside the door, she fires twice more. A flash of
lightning is followed by a drum roll of thunder.* MAX *moves
forward to the centre of the stage, aghast, for once
completely at a loss.*

20: THE HOUSE ON SUNSET

*The lights come up on the cold dawn of the opening scene.
The garden is now visible, bathed in an eerie glow, disrupted
by the blue lights of the patrol cars.* JOE's *body floats, face
down, in the pool. The entrance hall of the house is crowded
with reporters, police, newsreel crews with their cameras, all
fired with eager anticipation.* MAX *moves around the various
groups, consulting with policemen and cameramen.
Suddenly, all movement stops and all heads rise:* NORMA *has
emerged from her room on to the landing. She's dressed in
some strange approximation of a Salome costume and she's
still holding the revolver. There's an atmosphere of extreme
apprehension below. One of the uniformed* POLICEMEN *has
brought out his gun;* MAX *leans over to talk to the Head of
Homicide, a plainclothes detective.*
NORMA *is clearly disorientated, in a world of her own,
moving, lost and bewildered, around the landing, letting out,
unaccompanied by the orchestra, old broken phrases of song.)*

NORMA
   This was dawn.
   I don't know why I'm frightened.
   Silent music starts to play.
   Happy New Year, darling.
   If you're with me, next year will be . . .
   Next year will be . . .
   They bring in his head on a silver tray,
   She kisses his mouth . . .

She kisses his mouth . . .
Mad about the boy!
They'll say Norma's back at last!
(*By now,* MAX *has advanced to a position about halfway up the staircase.* NORMA *suddenly seems to come to herself. She looks at* MAX, *completely at a loss.*)

MAX
Madame, the cameras have arrived.

NORMA
Max, where am I?

MAX
This is the staircase of the palace
And they're waiting for your dance.

NORMA
Of course,
Now I remember:
I was so frightened I might fall . . .

MAX
You are the greatest star of all!
(*She starts down the stairs;* MAX *cups a hand to his mouth and springs into action.*)

MAX
Lights!
(*The portable lights flare up. In addition, there's the flash of countless flashbulbs.* NORMA *reacts, her eyes widen, she drapes the scarf around her shoulder.*)

MAX
Cameras!
(*The whirr and grind of the old-fashioned Movietone cameras.*)

MAX
Action!
(*And so, as the music swells,* NORMA *descends the staircase, waving her arms in some strange rendition of Salome's approach to the throne. However, halfway down,*

she suddenly comes to a halt and begins to speak.)

NORMA

I can't go on with the scene: I'm too happy. Do you mind if
I say a few words, Mr DeMille? I can't tell you how
wonderful it is to be back in the studio making a picture. I
promise you I'll never desert you again.

I've spent so many mornings
Just trying to resist you.
I'm trembling now
You can't know how
I've missed you.
Could I stop my hand from shaking?
Has there ever been a moment
With so much to live for?

This is my life. It always will be. There is nothing else. Just
us and the cameras and all you wonderful people out there
in the dark. And now, Mr DeMille, I'm ready for my
close-up.

(*She continues to advance down the staircase. The
policemen and journalists fall back to let her through and,
as she moves inexorably downstage, the lights begin to
narrow in and focus on her devastated features.*)

This time I'm staying,
I'm staying for good.
I'll be back,
Where I was born to be.
With one look
I'll be me.

(*Darkness.*)